CQR Pocke
American Government

Protections in the Bill of Rights

Amendment	Right or Provision
1st	Religious freedom
	Establishment clause
	Free exercise clause
	Free expression
	Right to free speech
	Freedom of the press
	Right to assembly
	Right to petition government
2nd	Right to bear arms
3rd	Consent to quarter soldiers
4th	Rights of the accused: Investigation stage
	Search and seizure clause
	Warrants require probable cause
5th	Rights of the accused: Arrest stage
	Grand jury guarantee
	No double jeopardy
	Right against self-incrimination
	Due process guarantee
	Takings clause
6th	Rights of the accused: Trial stage
	Right to a speedy, public trial
	Right to an impartial jury
	Right to be informed of charges
	Right to be confronted by accusers
	Subpoena power
	Right to counsel
7th	Right to trial by jury
8th	Rights of the accused: Penalty stage
	No excessive bail
	No cruel and unusual punishment
9th	Retains other rights for the people
10th	Un-delegated powers left to states or people

CQR Pocket Guide
American Government

HOW A BILL BECOMES A LAW

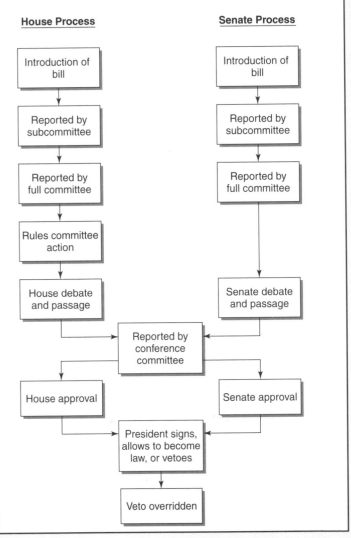

House Process

- Introduction of bill
- Reported by subcommittee
- Reported by full committee
- Rules committee action
- House debate and passage

Senate Process

- Introduction of bill
- Reported by subcommittee
- Reported by full committee
- Senate debate and passage

- Reported by conference committee

- House approval
- Senate approval

- President signs, allows to become law, or vetoes

- Veto overridden

For more information about Wiley,
call 1-800-762-2974.

CliffsQuickReview™
American
Government

By Paul Soifer, Ph.D.
Abraham Hoffman, Ph.D.
D. Stephen Voss, Ph.D.

Wiley Publishing, Inc.

About the Author

Paul Soifer holds a Ph.D. in history from Pennsylvania State University. He has more than a decade of experience teaching American history at the college level and is currently chair of the History Department at Yeshiva University High Schools of Los Angeles.

Abraham Hoffman has taught Advanced Placement U.S. History since 1982 in the Los Angeles Unified School District. He has served four terms as an AP reader for the U.S. History exam.

D. Stephen Voss, a specialist in voting behavior, is Assistant Professor of Political Science at the University of Kentucky. He received his doctorate from Harvard University.

Publisher's Acknowledgments

Editorial

Editor: Christine Meloy Beck

Acquisitions Editor: Sherry Gomoll

Editorial Assistant: Jennifer Young

Production

Indexer: York Production Services, Inc.

Proofreader: York Production Services, Inc.

Wiley Publishing, Inc., Indianapolis Composition Services

CliffsQuickReview™ *American Government*
Published by:
Wiley Publishing, Inc.
909 Third Avenue
New York, NY 10022
www.wiley.com

Published by Wiley Publishing, Inc., New York, NY
Published simultaneously in Canada

Table of Contents

INTRODUCTION

Many high school and college students expect that their American Government class will be a piece of cake. After all, many have lived under the American system all their lives. Unfortunately, these folks often face a rude awakening. American Government classes often follow a hectic pace, are packed with complicated facts and stories, and usually require students to analyze information at a greater depth than anything expected of them before. The whole thing can be terribly bewildering without assistance.

Nor are high school and college students the only ones who find themselves struggling to understand American politics. Regular citizens commonly decide that they ought to know a bit more about the government that rules them, but they find that news coverage of politics seldom explains enough to really understand what is going on. And many people who come to the United States from foreign countries, whether as immigrants or as international students, struggle to understand the American way of running a government, which can seem so alien to their own.

The book you now hold in your hand is intended to help out, whether you are a student under pressure, an interested citizen trying to brush up, or a recent arrival trying to understand this new land in which you find yourself. It is not a textbook so much as a valuable guidebook. It provides an overview of the history, institutions, practices, and policies of the American government—but in a convenient presentation, with plain words and useful formats, so that you can use your time efficiently. It provides the resources you need to test and reinforce what you have learned. And it points you in the right direction if you want, or need, more information about the subject covered inside. You will find CliffsQuickReview *American Government* a valuable addition to your learning tools.

Why You Need This Book

Can you answer yes to any of these questions?

- Do you need to review the fundamentals of American government fast?

- Do you need a course supplement to help you understand how government works?

- Do you need a concise, comprehensive reference on American politics?

If so, then CliffsQuickReview *American Government* is for you!

How to Use This Book

You can use this book in any way that fits your personal style for study and review—you decide what works best with your needs. You can either read the book from cover to cover or just look for the information you want and put it back on the shelf for later. Here are just a few ways you can search for topics:

- Use the Pocket Guide to find essential information, such as an overview of the Bill of Rights.

- Look for areas of interest in the book's Table of Contents, or use the index to find specific topics.

- Flip through the book looking for subject areas at the top of each page.

- Get a glimpse of what you'll gain from a chapter by reading through the Chapter Check-In at the beginning of each chapter.

- Use the Chapter Checkout at the end of each chapter to gauge your grasp of the important information you need to know.

- Test your knowledge more completely in the CQR Review and look for additional sources of information in the CQR Resource Center.

- Use the glossary to find key terms fast. This book defines new terms and concepts where they first appear in the chapter. If a word is bold-faced, you can find a more complete definition in the book's glossary.

- Or flip through the book until you find what you're looking for—we organized this book to gradually build on key concepts.

Visit Our Web Site

A great resource, www.cliffsnotes.com features review materials, valuable Internet links, quizzes, and more to enhance your learning. The site also features timely articles and tips, plus downloadable versions of many CliffsNotes books.

When you stop by our site, don't hesitate to share your thoughts about this book or any Hungry Minds product. Just click the Talk to Us button. We welcome your feedback!

Chapter 1

THE CONSTITUTION

Chapter Check-In

❏ Tracing the events that led to the writing of the U.S. Constitution

❏ Reviewing the compromises that were necessary for the Constitution to be ratified

❏ Understanding the various concepts and provisions embodied by the Constitution

The United States was not the first country to have a "constitution." People in England, the mother country of the American colonies, also used that term to describe the rules structuring their government. But to the British, the constitution was not a single document or code. It was not something they could print on expensive paper or preserve in a museum. It was simply all the various laws and customs that determined how their government was "constituted"—how it normally behaved.

Americans of the Revolutionary War era took this concept to a new level. Many saw the relationship between rulers and ruled as a contract, one that gave citizens responsibilities but also placed obligations on their leaders. There were things the government was permitted to do, and other things that were forbidden. But how would leaders know their privileges and their limits without some kind of guidance? How could citizens know whether their government was violating the bargain, unless a list of Do's and Don'ts existed somewhere?

The Constitution of the United States evolved to fulfill this desire for a binding contract. It enumerated (listed) the powers available to the national government and explicitly forbid other actions (a list that grew with the first several amendments). The U.S. Constitution therefore defined the basic structure of national government, but it did so in a fundamentally new way—because it was a *written* code that the *government lacked authority to change.* For this reason, the U.S. Constitution is considered the oldest working constitution in the world.

The Continental Congress

Twelve of the 13 colonies sent representatives to the **First Continental Congress,** which met in Philadelphia in September 1774. At that meeting, resolutions and a statement of rights and principles were adopted that still looked to a peaceful settlement with Great Britain. The **Second Continental Congress** convened in May 1775, after the battles of Lexington and Concord. Without legal authority to do so, the Second Continental Congress assumed governmental functions. It established a postal system, created a navy and marine corps, negotiated treaties with the Native Americans, and looked for allies overseas. Most important, the Congress formally voted to declare independence from Great Britain.

The Declaration of Independence

Written chiefly by Thomas Jefferson, the Declaration of Independence (adopted July 4, 1776, by the Second Continental Congress) provided the specific reasons for the break with Great Britain. Its philosophical justification drew heavily from John Locke's *Two Treatises of Government* (1690). Locke argued that people have **natural rights**—"Life, Liberty, and the pursuit of Happiness," in Jefferson's words—that cannot be taken away. Governments, which get their power from the consent of the governed, are created to protect these rights. When a government fails to do so, the people have a right to abolish it and create a new form of government.

State constitutions

The idea that the people were the source of power was also included in many of the new state constitutions. Having just rebelled against the king, most states severely limited executive power. The legislatures were supreme, and in many instances not only made the laws but also appointed the governors, judges, and other officials. Individual liberties were usually safeguarded. The state legislatures continued to enjoy considerable authority under the Articles of Confederation.

The Articles of Confederation

The **Articles of Confederation** were adopted by the Second Continental Congress on November 15, 1777, but did not become effective until March 1, 1781, when they were finally approved by all 13 states. Under the Articles, the national government consisted of a **unicameral** (one-house) legislature (often called the *Confederation Congress*); there was no national executive or judiciary. Delegates to Congress were appointed by the state legislatures, and each state had one vote. Congress had the authority to declare war, develop foreign policy, coin money, regulate Native American affairs in the territories, run the post office, borrow money, and appoint army and navy officers. Quite significantly, however, all powers not specifically delegated to Congress belonged to the states.

Weaknesses of the Articles of Confederation

Congress did not have the direct power to tax or to regulate interstate and foreign trade. It could only ask the states for money with no means to compel payment, and the states had the right to impose their own duties on imports, which caused havoc with commerce. Congress had no authority to raise an army on its own and had to requisition troops from the states. All major policy issues—war and peace, treaties, the appropriation of funds—required the approval of nine states. The Articles reflected the nation's concern about executive power; however, the lack of an executive meant there was no effective leadership. A unanimous vote of the states, acting through their legislatures, was necessary to amend the Articles.

Calls to strengthen the national government

The need for a stronger national government was aired by the representatives of five states, including Alexander Hamilton and James Madison, at the **Annapolis Convention** (September 1786). The inability of Congress to deal with **Shay's Rebellion** (winter of 1786–1787), a revolt of debtor farmers in western Massachusetts, made the shortcomings of the Articles clear. In February 1787, Congress agreed to hold another meeting "for the sole and express purpose of revising the Articles of Confederation."

The Constitutional Convention

Fifty-five delegates from 12 states (Rhode Island did not participate) met in Philadelphia in May 1787. While authorized only to "revise" the Articles of Confederation, the participants moved quickly to develop a new structure for the government.

The Virginia Plan

The early debates centered on a proposal by James Madison known as the **Virginia Plan.** Supported by the large states, it called for a **bicameral** (two-house) legislature empowered to make laws. The lower house was elected by voters in each state, and the upper house was chosen by the lower house from candidates nominated by the state legislatures. Representation in both houses was based on population. The executive was chosen by the legislature for one term and was responsible for executing all laws. The legislature also appointed the judges to one or more supreme courts and lower national courts. A Council of Revision made up of the executive and judges could veto laws passed by the legislature or the states; a vote by both houses was needed to override a veto by the Council.

The New Jersey Plan

The small states supported a less radical departure from the Articles of Confederation. The **New Jersey Plan** kept the one-house legislature, with its powers expanded to include raising revenue and regulating commerce. Each state had one vote, and the members were chosen by the state legislatures. A multiperson executive elected by the legislature was proposed. The executives, who were removable by action of the majority of the governors, also appointed judges to the Supreme Court. Laws passed by the legislature were binding on the states, and the multiperson executive was authorized to compel obedience to the law.

The Great Compromise

The New Jersey Plan was rejected, but the apportionment of representation in Congress continued to divide the Convention. The large states wanted **proportional representation** (by population), and the small states demanded equal representation (one state, one vote). The **Great Compromise** (also known as the **Connecticut Compromise**) provided that seats in the House of Representatives would be apportioned according to the population of each state, with members elected directly by the people. In the Senate, each state would have two senators, voting independently, chosen by their legislatures.

Decisions on slavery

Slaves were a significant percentage of the population in the Southern states. The issue of whether or how to count slaves was resolved by a formula used by Congress in 1783. For purposes of representation in the House and assessing direct taxes to the states, population was determined by adding the "whole number of free persons" and "three-fifths of all other persons." The phrase "all other persons" meant slaves. In addition to adopting the **Three-Fifths Compromise,** the delegates to the Convention allowed the slave trade to continue by denying Congress the power to prohibit it before 1808 and agreed that fugitive slaves should be returned to their masters.

Compromise over the presidency

The Convention accepted a one-person executive but hotly debated how the president should be elected (by Congress or the people) and the term of office. The solution was the **Electoral College.** The legislatures of each state chose electors equal to their total number of representatives in Congress. The electors then voted for two people, one of whom could not be from their state. The individual who received the most votes became president and the person with the next highest total became vice president. In the event of a tie, the House of Representatives decided the election and each state had one vote. The president's term of office was set at four years, and no express limit was put on the number of terms.

Key Concepts in the Constitution

The Constitution, which was approved by the delegates to the Convention on September 17, 1787, established a republican form of government, explained the organization of that government, and outlined the federal system.

Republican form of government

The Constitution established the United States as a republic in which power ultimately is in the hands of the people and is exercised by their elected representatives. The Republic was not a democracy in the modern sense, however. The framers of the Constitution, many reluctantly, accepted slavery. There were property qualifications for voting, and some states denied the right to vote to religious minorities. Women did not get to vote in the national elections until 1920 (Nineteenth Amendment). The original draft of the Constitution did not include protection of basic civil liberties.

The organization of government

The government's functions are divided among three branches: the legislative branch that makes the laws (Congress), the executive branch that carries out the laws (president), and the judicial branch that interprets the laws (courts). This division is known as the **separation of powers.** In addition, under the system of **checks and balances,** the powers of one branch of government are limited by the powers given to another branch. Congress makes laws, but the president can veto legislation. Congress can override a president's veto with a two-thirds vote of both houses (a check on a check). While the president appoints judges to the Supreme Court, the Senate can reject an appointee through its power to give "advice and consent."

The federal system

Federalism means the division of power between the national government and the states. The Constitution does not clearly define, however, the areas in which these powers are exercised. Keeping in mind that the framers were determined to strengthen the national government, it is not surprising that the powers belonging to the states were left vague.

Summary of the Constitution

The Constitution was a spare document, providing few details about how the U.S. government would run itself. It explained the rough organization of the three branches, how they would interact with the states, and how the document could be amended. Filling in the details was left to future leaders.

Article I

The longest article in the Constitution vests legislative power in the Senate and the House of Representatives. It describes the organization of Congress and lists its specific powers, known as **enumerated** or **delegated powers.** Through the **necessary and proper clause** (also called the **elastic clause**), Congress can make laws needed to carry out its enumerated powers. Article I also lists the powers denied to Congress and the states.

Article II

This article deals with the executive branch and describes the election of the president (and vice president), the qualifications for holding the office, and the procedures if a president can no longer serve. The powers of the president include serving as commander in chief of the army and navy, making treaties, and, with the "advice and consent of the Senate," appointing ambassadors, officials, and Supreme Court justices. The president is required to periodically report to Congress on the state of the union, can propose legislation, and can call Congress into special session.

Article III

This article established the Supreme Court and authorizes Congress to establish lower federal courts. The types of cases the courts have jurisdiction over are given, and a provision is made for the right to trial by jury. While not specifically stated, the power of the courts to declare a law unconstitutional is implied.

Article IV

The full faith and credit clause requires that the legislative and judicial actions of one state be honored by the other states. Additionally, a citizen of any state has the same privileges as citizens of all the other states. Article IV also provides for adding new states to the union, guarantees each state a republican form of government, and ensures protection against invasion or domestic violence.

Article V

The process for amending the Constitution is described. The states are responsible for ratifying amendments.

Article VI

The Constitution, the laws of the United States, and treaties entered into by the United States are the supreme law of the land. This is known as the **supremacy clause.**

Article VII

Approval by conventions of nine of the states was required to ratify the Constitution.

The Debate over Ratification

The debate over ratification was waged in the newspapers, through pamphlets, and on the floor of the state conventions, where the vote was often close. Those who favored the strong national government provided for in the Constitution called themselves the **Federalists;** their opponents became the **Antifederalists.**

The Antifederalists

The Antifederalists believed that the Constitution gave too much power to the central government and left the states with too little. Strong proponents of individual liberty, they vigorously criticized the omission of a bill of rights, which was included in many state constitutions. Some considered the ratification process itself illegal, because unanimous consent from the states was required to amend the Articles of Confederation.

The Federalists

The case for the Constitution was effectively presented in a series of newspaper articles that were written by Alexander Hamilton, John Jay, and James Madison, collectively known as **The Federalist Papers.** The Federalists argued that the new government would not be dominated by any one group and that there were adequate safeguards to protect individuals and the states.

On June 21, 1788, New Hampshire became the ninth state to ratify the Constitution. Two key states—Virginia and New York—gave their approval during the next month. An important factor in swaying the state conventions was a commitment from the Federalists to add a bill of rights after ratification.

The Amendment Process and Bill of Rights

The Constitution (Article V) provides that amendments can be proposed either by Congress, with a two-thirds vote of both houses, or by a national convention requested by two-thirds of the state legislatures. Amendments are ratified by three-fourths of the state legislatures or by conventions in three-fourths of the states. Only the Twenty-first Amendment, which repealed Prohibition in 1933, was adopted by state conventions.

The Bill of Rights

Congress proposed 12 amendments in September 1789; three-fourths of the states approved ten of them in December 1791, creating the Bill of Rights. The following list summarizes the Bill of Rights:

- Prohibits the establishment of a state religion and protects freedom of the press and speech and the rights to assemble and petition the government (Amendment I)

- Guarantees the right to keep and bear arms in the context of a state militia (Amendment II)

- Prohibits the stationing of troops in homes without consent (Amendment III)

■ Protects against unreasonable searches and seizures and requires **probable cause** for search warrants (Amendment IV)

■ Establishes a **grand jury** to bring indictments in capital or serious cases, protects against **double jeopardy** (a person cannot be tried twice for the same crime) and **self-incrimination** (individuals cannot be forced to testify against themselves), and guarantees **due process** and **eminent domain** (compensation must be paid for private property taken for public use) (Amendment V)

■ Guarantees the right to a speedy trial by an impartial jury in criminal cases, to be informed about charges, and to have representation by counsel (Amendment VI)

■ Provides for trial by jury in most civil cases (Amendment VII)

■ Prohibits excessive bail or fines and cruel and unusual punishments (Amendment VIII)

■ Does not deny people any rights not specifically mentioned in the Constitution (Amendment IX)

■ Gives to the states or the people powers not granted to Congress or denied to the states (Amendment X)

Subsequent amendments to the Constitution

Since the enactment of the Bill of Rights, the amendment process has been used sparingly. While numerous amendments have been proposed in Congress, only a handful have gone to the states for action. An additional 17 amendments to the Constitution have been ratified over the last 200 years; six proposals failed to win enough support—most recently, the Equal Rights Amendment, strongly backed by women's groups, and an amendment to give the District of Columbia full representation in Congress. The country has used the amendment process once to promote a particular social policy; Amendment XVIII (1919) prohibited the manufacture and sale of intoxicating liquors but was repealed in 1933 (Amendment XXI). The other amendments either address how the government operates or expand equality. Table 1-1 provides a brief summary of the amendments added to the Constitution since the enactment of the Bill of Rights.

Table 1-1   Amendments to the Constitution, 1798–1992

Amendment	Date	Subject
XI	1798	A state cannot be sued by individuals in another state
XII	1804	Electors cast separate votes for president and vice president
XIII	1865	Slavery abolished
XIV	1868	Due process and equal protection of the law given to all persons born or naturalized in the U.S.
XV	1870	Right to vote cannot be denied because of race, color, or previous condition of slavery
XVI	1913	Federal income tax established
XVII	1913	Direct election of senators
XVIII	1919	Prohibition
XIX	1920	Women given the right to vote
XX	1933	Dates of presidential inauguration and opening of Congress
XXI	1933	Prohibition repealed
XXII	1951	President limited to two terms
XXIII	1961	Citizens of District of Columbia given right to vote for president
XXIV	1964	Prohibits poll tax for voting
XXV	1967	Succession of president or vice president
XXVI	1971	Minimum voting age set at 18
XXVII	1992	Limits on when pay raises for members of Congress can be enacted

Chapter Checkout

Q&A

1. Which clause of the U.S. Constitution is known as the *elastic clause* because of the expansive powers it allows the Congress?

   a. The supremacy clause
   b. The necessary and proper clause
   c. The full faith and credit clause
   d. The enumerated clause
   e. The Santa clause

2. Which of the following was NOT a problem with the U.S. government under the Articles of Confederation?

   a. States could impose import taxes on goods brought in from other states.
   b. The Confederation Congress had no authority to raise an army on its own.
   c. Major policy changes required the approval of $9/13$ of the delegations.
   d. The Articles could not be amended unless every state approved.
   e. The President under the Articles was so strong that he resembled a king.
   f. Each state could choose how much to pay in national taxes.

3. What reasons did the Antifederalists give for opposing the U.S. Constitution?

Answers: 1. b **2.** e **3.** Made national government too strong, lacked a bill of rights, used illegal ratification process.

Critical Thinking

1. The Bill of Rights contained ten amendments to the U.S. Constitution. Only 17 more amendments have been added to the document since then, and of those, only a handful describe new "rights," despite dramatic changes in American society over the last 200 years. Propose a new amendment for the Constitution that establishes a critical "right" not currently protected by the document and explain why this "right" ought to be protected.

Chapter 2

FEDERALISM

Chapter Check-In

❑ Considering how the national government should relate to the states

❑ Exploring the role played by different branches of government in shaping that relationship

❑ Understanding the political implications of changes in the federal structure

Federalism refers to a type of government in which the power is divided between the national government and other governmental units. It contrasts with a **unitary government,** in which a central authority holds the power, and a **confederation,** in which states, for example, are clearly dominant.

While the Constitution addressed only the relationship between the federal government and the states, the American people are under multiple jurisdictions. A person not only pays his or her federal income tax but also may pay state and city income taxes as well. Property taxes are collected by counties and are used to provide law enforcement, build new schools, and maintain local roads.

Concepts of Federalism

Throughout the 20th century, the power of the federal government expanded considerably through legislation and court decisions. While much recent political debate has centered on returning power to the states, the relationship between the federal government and the states has been argued over for most of the history of the United States.

The constitutional framework

Although the Constitution sets up a federal system, nowhere does it define what federalism is. As you can read in Chapter 1, however, the framers of the Constitution were determined to create a strong national government and address the shortcomings of the Articles of Confederation, which allowed the states too much power. In terms of the balance of power between the federal government and the states, the Constitution clearly favors the federal government.

The powers specifically given to the federal government are not as relevant to the expansion of its authority as the Constitution's more general provisions; that is, Congress is to provide for the general welfare (preamble) and ". . . make all laws which shall be necessary and proper. . . ." (Article I, Section 8). In the Constitution as ratified, there is no similar broad grant of powers to the states. It emphasized what states cannot do (Article I, Section 10) and gave them authority in just a few areas—namely, establishing voter qualifications and setting up the mechanics of congressional elections. This reduction in power was corrected through the Tenth Amendment, which reserved to the states or the people all powers either not specifically delegated to the national government or specifically denied to the states. The language in the general welfare and elastic clauses and the Tenth Amendment is vague enough to allow widely different interpretations. Because both federal and state governments can turn to the Constitution for support, it is not surprising that different concepts of federalism have emerged.

Dual federalism

Dual federalism looks at the federal system as a sort of "layer cake," with each layer of government performing the tasks that make the most sense for that level.

The initial framing and ratification of the Constitution reflected this theory. Even those people supporting a stronger national government proposed that powers in the federal government be distinct and limited, with certain tasks enumerated for the national government in the Constitution and the remaining tasks left to the state governments. Because this theory leaves each government supreme within its own sphere of operations, it is also sometimes called *dual sovereignty.*

One more-extreme outgrowth of this theory is the idea of **states' rights,** which holds that because the national government is not allowed to infringe on spheres left to state government, doing so violates the states' constitutional rights (especially the Tenth Amendment, which specifically reserves undelegated powers for the states). Federal government action in those spheres represents an unlawful seizure of power by one level of government at the expense of another. This view has historically been popular in the South, where it was viewed as preventing national government interference in the region's race relations, but it has been invoked elsewhere as well.

The problem with taking dual federalism this far is figuring out who defines where one layer ends and the next layer starts. Before the Civil War, some voices said that, to protect their rights, states could secede from the Union or declare national laws that affect them null and void—but those arguments are no longer taken seriously. Instead, the U.S. Supreme Court resolves disputes within the federal structure, and because the Court is a national institution, it rarely favors the states.

Cooperative federalism

The theory of **cooperative federalism** emerged during the New Deal, when the power of the federal government grew in response to the Great Depression. It does not recognize a clear distinction between the functions of the states and Washington, and it emphasizes that there are many areas in which their responsibilities overlap. For example, drug enforcement involves federal agents, state troopers, and local police. The federal government supplies funds for education, but the state and local school boards choose curriculum and set qualifications for teachers. (Interestingly, attempts to set national standards for students in certain subjects have raised concerns of federal intrusion.) The notion of overlapping jurisdictions is expressed by the term *marble-cake federalism.*

Cooperative federalism takes a very loose view of the elastic clause that allows power to flow through federal government. It is a more accurate model of how the federal system has worked over much of U.S. history.

Defining Federal–State Relations

Federalism is a fluid concept. Historically, the relationship between the two levels of government has been defined by the courts, Congress, and funding policies.

The role of the courts

Questions concerning the respective powers of the states and the federal government are constitutional, and the courts must address them. Early Supreme Court decisions reflected the views of Chief Justice John Marshall, who personally favored a strong national government. In defining commerce in the broadest possible terms in *Gibbons v. Ogden* (1824), he argued that Congress's power to regulate interstate commerce could be "exercised to its utmost extent." Marshall's interpretation of the **commerce clause** has provided a means to enforce civil rights laws and regulate wages, working conditions, and other areas that seem at first glance far removed from federal jurisdiction. At the same time, however, he believed the Bill of Rights imposed no restrictions to the states.

Throughout most of the 19th century and on into the 1930s, the Supreme Court did not follow Marshall's lead; it was reluctant to allow an expansion of federal power at the expense of the states. As the makeup of the Court changed with the appointments made by President Franklin Roosevelt, so did the direction of its decisions. In the areas of civil liberties and civil rights in particular, the Supreme Court and the lower federal courts have set national standards that states and municipalities are obligated to follow. Through their interpretation of the due process and equal protection clauses of the Fourteenth Amendment, they have brought about a significant transfer of power from the states to the federal government. This amendment, along with the Fifteenth and the Twenty-fourth, has largely restricted the authority of the states to determine who can vote and where they cast their ballots. The courts have directed how state and local authorities draw their congressional, legislative, and school-board district boundaries.

The role of Congress

Legislation can compel states either directly or indirectly to take action they otherwise might not take. Again, civil rights provide a pertinent example. The 1965 Voting Rights Act intruded on the constitutional power of the states to set voter qualifications by challenging the literacy tests and poll tax that were used in the South to get around the Fifteenth Amendment.

A wide range of environmental laws establishes requirements for air and water pollution control and the disposal of hazardous wastes to which states and municipalities must adhere. These are examples of *mandates*.

Congress may also threaten to cut off funds if states do not implement a particular policy. Although a law forcing the states to establish 21 as the minimum drinking age or 55 miles per hour as the maximum highway speed might be unconstitutional, Congress can and did threaten to cut off federal highway funds to states that did not comply with the two limits. This is known as a *condition of aid*.

The role of funding policies

The most powerful tool the federal government has in its relations with the states is money. A *grant-in-aid* is funding provided by the federal government to the states or municipalities. The earliest federal grants were land. Under the Morrill Act (1862), the states received large tracts of land for the specific purpose of establishing agricultural and mechanical colleges (still known as **land-grant colleges**).

A **categorical grant** earmarks funds for a specific purpose. The two types of categorical grants are project and formula grants. A **project grant** is awarded on the basis of competitive applications; money from the National Institutes of Health or the National Endowment for the Humanities is awarded in this manner. While many project grants go to individuals, **formula grants** go to states and municipalities that meet the requirements described in the legislation. Depending on what the grant is for, factors such as the age, education, and income level of the population, the number of miles of highway, or the unemployment rate might be relevant to qualifying for aid.

A **block grant** is given for more general purposes than categorical grants— say, mental health, community services, mass transit, or job training—and state and local governments have a great deal of flexibility in how the money is actually spent. A county may decide to upgrade its buses rather than build a light rail system, for example. This does not mean, however, that strings are not attached to block grants. Recipients are bound by federal mandates. The county upgrading its buses may be required to buy a certain percentage of them from a minority-owned business or hire additional drivers from a training program for those on welfare.

Recent Trends in Federalism

A high-water mark in the shift of power to the federal government came during the administration of President Lyndon Johnson (1963–1969). This fact is not surprising because Johnson himself was a New Dealer and had faith in the ability of the federal government to address the country's problems. His administration pushed through major civil rights legislation as well as the programs of the Great Society, which included the "War on Poverty" and Medicare. Johnson's one important innovation was to direct more money straight to the cities and give nongovernmental agencies, such as community groups, a role in deciding how the federal resources would be used. The number of grants increased significantly, as did the size of the bureaucracy needed to manage them.

Richard Nixon and the New Federalism

Every president since Johnson has stated that the federal government is too large and that power should be returned to the states. Richard Nixon's attempt to do so was called the **New Federalism.** Its key component was special revenue sharing, under which tax money was returned to the states and cities. They could decide which of their own programs needed an infusion of federal dollars. In addition, categorical grants were combined into block grants.

Nixon's approach to federalism was not completely consistent. His administration saw the creation of the Occupational Health and Safety Administration (OSHA) and passage of the Clean Air Act, both of which imposed additional federal mandates on state and local governments. Even though revenue-sharing funds were largely unrestricted, accepting the money meant following the same federal requirements that applied to block grants.

Federalism under Reagan

Ronald Reagan came into the White House committed to giving the states more power. In practice, this commitment meant reducing federal domestic spending and encouraging the states to take over programs that had been Washington's responsibility. The states not only had to administer the programs, but they also had to find new sources of revenue to pay for them. The administration proposed, for example, that the federal government assume all costs for Medicare while the states take over food stamps and other direct welfare payments.

As a result of budget cuts, there was a sharp decline in federal aid to the states during the Reagan years. The states and municipalities responded by raising taxes, privatizing services (for example, contracting with private companies for trash collection), and cutting programs. Many states turned to lotteries to raise general revenues or to help fund specific programs such as education.

Ongoing mandates

If the relationship between the federal government and the states is to fundamentally change, it will come about through legislation. Recent laws, however, have added to the federal mandates. Every time Congress expands the eligibility for Medicaid or tightens the standards on air pollution, the costs to states and localities go up. Another example: No money was provided in the Americans with Disabilities Act to pay for retrofitting buildings to make them accessible to the handicapped.

Unfunded mandates became a hot political issue in the early 1990s. The issue was not only legislative requirements but also the consequences of what were perceived to be failed national policies. For example, Governor Pete Wilson of California, who ran briefly for the 1996 Republican nomination for president, argued that the states should not have to pay for the inability of the federal government to control the nation's borders. California's expenses for illegal aliens and their children include welfare and public education.

Where Americans stand

Polls indicate that in a comparatively short time, there has been a significant change in the way Americans view the relationship between the states and the federal government. In 1994, almost three-quarters of the population believed that the federal government was too powerful. This number contrasts sharply with 1987 data, which showed fewer than half of all Americans taking this position. Less than 20 percent thought the balance between the states and the federal government was about right in 1994, whereas the largest group of people was satisfied with the balance just seven years earlier. The 1994 poll also showed that Americans viewed state and local government as better equipped than Washington to handle a variety of domestic issues ranging from crime to welfare to transportation. Even though Americans were roughly split on who could best tackle health care, President Bill Clinton's reform proposals failed to gain much headway, in part because they were seen as increasing the federal government's role.

This anti-Washington sentiment was a factor in the Republicans' gaining control of both houses of Congress in 1994. The House Republicans put forward their own legislative agenda known as the *Contract With America,* which stressed returning power to the states. One of the concrete results was legislation that limited new federal mandates unless money was also provided to cover them. In the latest welfare reform and immigration laws, the benefits that illegal immigrants are entitled to were curtailed as well.

Chapter Checkout

Q&A

1. In the middle 1990s, three-quarters of the American population apparently believed that more power should be given to the
   a. state and local governments
   b. national government
   c. U.S. Supreme Court
   d. health care initiative established by President Clinton
   e. Trilateral Commission

2. Chief Justice John Marshall's expansive interpretation of the _____ clause in *Gibbons v. Ogden* eventually led to wide congressional authority in areas such as civil rights and labor law.

3. True or False: Congress is unable to coerce states into adopting particular policies by cutting off their funds for related programs.

Answers: 1. a **2.** Commerce **3.** F (unfunded mandates)

Chapter 3

CONGRESS

Chapter Check-In

❑ Reviewing how Congress is organized

❑ Tracing the law-making process

❑ Understanding why representatives vote as they do

Congress is divided into two chambers, the Senate and the House of Representatives. The Senate is sometimes called the "upper" chamber and the House the "lower" chamber because the Founders thought that different sorts of people would be elected to these two bodies. House members face elections every two years in smaller districts, so the Founders thought that representatives would be closer to the people. In contrast, Senators were originally chosen by state legislatures, and with elections every six years and steeper eligibility requirements, the Founders believed that the Senate would serve as a voice for the nation's wealthy and established interests.

To a certain extent, the Founders correctly predicted differences between the two chambers. The Senate is more deliberative, with strict rules to encourage debate, and it follows decorous norms of behavior like those of some exclusive club. The House is a bit rowdier, allowing confrontational leaders like former House Speaker Newt Gingrich to rise in influence.

But in other ways the Founders were mistaken. Senators have been directly elected by voters since the Seventeenth Amendment passed in 1913 and are much more likely to lose reelection campaigns—so they must work harder to curry favor if they want to keep their positions. Members of the House, by contrast, seldom lose their reelection bids unless they have been marked by scandal or their districts have changed. They are more insulated from the popular passions that America's Founders feared they would express.

The Powers of Congress

Under the Constitution, Congress has both specific and implied powers. These powers have been expanded through the amendment process as well as by Congress's own legislative action. Moreover, both houses are granted authority in certain areas.

Specific powers

Congress is given 27 specific powers under Article I, Section 8, of the Constitution. These are commonly known as the **enumerated powers,** and they cover such areas as the rights to collect taxes, regulate foreign and domestic commerce, coin money, declare war, support an army and navy, and establish lower federal courts. In addition, Congress can admit new states to the Union (Article IV, Section 3), propose amendments to the Constitution (Article V), collect federal income taxes (Sixteenth Amendment), and enforce protection and extension of civil rights (Thirteenth, Fifteenth, Nineteenth, Twenty-third, Twenty-fourth, and Twenty-sixth Amendments).

Implied powers

Implied powers are not stated directly in the Constitution. They derive from the right of Congress to make all laws "necessary and proper" to carry out its enumerated powers. Located at the end of Article I, Section 8, this sentence is often called the **elastic clause** because it stretches the authority of Congress. The Supreme Court upheld the concept of implied powers in the landmark case **McCulloch v. Maryland** (1819), ruling that the federal government had the right to establish a national bank under the power delegated to Congress to borrow money and control commerce. A more recent example of implied powers is the **War Powers Act of 1973,** which limited the ability of the President to send American troops into combat without consulting and notifying Congress.

Limitations on the powers of Congress

The Constitution lists powers that are denied to Congress (Article I, Section 9). The Bill of Rights prohibits Congress from making laws that limit individual liberties. Under the system of checks and balances, the president can veto a law passed by Congress, or the Supreme Court can declare a law unconstitutional. Voters can ignore unpopular laws and press for their repeal, as happened with the Eighteenth Amendment establishing Prohibition.

The Organization of Congress

Congress consists of 100 senators (two from each state) and 435 members of the House of Representatives, a number that was fixed by the

Reapportionment Act of 1929. This act recognized that simply adding more seats to the House as the population grew would make it too unwieldy. Today, each congressperson represents approximately 570,000 people.

Congressional districts

Americans are known for their mobility, and over the years states have lost and gained population. After each federal census, which occurs every ten years, adjustments are made in the number of congressional districts. This process is known as **reapportionment.** In recent years, states in the West and Southwest have increased their representation in the House, while states in the Northeast and Midwest have lost seats.

Congressional district lines are usually drawn by the state legislatures (although the federal courts sometimes draw districts when the original plans lose a constitutional challenge). The majority party often tries to draw the boundaries to maximize the chances for its candidates to win elections. In 1812, Governor Elbridge Gerry of Massachusetts approved a bill creating such an oddly shaped district that his critics called it a "gerrymander"— a political amphibian with a malicious design. **Gerrymandering** now refers to the creating of any oddly shaped district designed to elect a representative of a particular political party or a particular ethnic group.

Members of Congress

For most of the nation's history, members of Congress have been mainly white males. Beginning with the civil rights movement of the 1960s, the number of ethnic minorities and women in Congress has increased. There has been less change in the occupational backgrounds of the representatives and senators. Many legislators are lawyers or businesspeople, or they have made a career of political life.

Once elected to office, members of Congress represent their constituents in different ways. Some consider themselves **delegates,** obligated to vote the way the majority of the people in their districts want. A congressperson or senator who takes this position makes every effort to stay in touch with voter public opinion through questionnaires or surveys and frequent trips back home. Others see themselves as **trustees** who, while taking the views of their constituents into account, use their own best judgment or their conscience to vote. President John Quincy Adams, who served ten terms in the House after he was defeated in the presidential election of 1828, is a classic example of a representative as trustee.

Members of Congress have a clear advantage over challengers who want to unseat them. Current members are **incumbents,** candidates for reelection who already hold the office. As such, they have name recognition because the people in the district or state know them. They can use the **franking privilege,** or free use of the mail, to send out newsletters informing their constituents about their views or asking for input. Incumbents traditionally have easier access to campaign funds and volunteers to generate votes. It is not surprising that 90 percent of incumbents are reelected. The situation is not static, however. Legislators run for other offices, and vacancies are created by death, retirement, and resignation. Although **term limits,** restricting the number of consecutive terms an individual can serve, were rejected by the Supreme Court, the idea continues to enjoy the support of voters who want to see more open contests.

Leadership in the House

The Speaker of the House of Representatives is the only presiding officer and traditionally has been the main spokesperson for the majority party in the House. The position is a very powerful one; the Speaker is third in line in presidential succession (after the president and vice president). The Speaker's real power comes from controlling the selection of committee chairs and committee members and the authority to set the order of business of the House.

The **majority floor leader** is second only to the Speaker. He or she comes from the political party that controls the House and is elected through a *caucus,* a meeting of the House party members. The majority leader presents the official position of the party on issues and tries to keep party members loyal to that position, which is not always an easy task. In the event that a minority party wins a majority of the seats in a congressional election, its minority leader usually becomes the majority leader.

The minority party in the House also has a leadership structure, topped by the **minority floor leader.** Whoever fills this elected position serves as the chief spokesperson and legislative strategist for the party and often works hard to win the support of moderate members of the opposition on particular votes. Although the minority leader has little formal power, it is an important job, especially because whoever holds it conventionally takes over the speakership if control of the House changes hands.

Leadership in the Senate

The Senate has a somewhat different leadership structure. The vice president is officially the presiding officer and is called the **president of the**

Senate. The vice president seldom appears in the Senate chamber in this role unless it appears that a crucial vote may end in a tie. In such instances, the vice president casts the tiebreaking vote.

To deal with day-to-day business, the Senate chooses the **president pro tempore.** This position is an honorary one and is traditionally given to the senator in the majority party who has the longest continuous service. Because the president pro tempore is a largely ceremonial office, the real work of presiding is done by many senators. As in the House, the Senate has majority and minority leaders. The majority leader exercises considerable political influence. One of the most successful majority leaders was Lyndon Johnson, who led the Senate from 1955 to 1961. His power of persuasion was legendary in getting fellow senators to go along with him on key votes.

In both the Senate and the House, the majority and minority party leadership selects **whips,** who see to it that party members are present for important votes. They also provide their colleagues with information needed to ensure party loyalty. Because there are so many members of Congress, whips are aided by numerous assistants.

The work of congressional committees

Much of the work of Congress is done in committees, where bills are introduced, hearings are held, and the first votes on proposed laws are taken. The committee structure allows Congress to research an area of public policy, to hear from interested parties, and to develop the expertise of its members. Committee membership reflects the party breakdown; the majority party has a majority of the seats on each committee, including the chair, who is usually chosen by **seniority** (years of consecutive service on the committee). Membership on a key committee may also be politically advantageous to a senator or representative.

Both houses have four types of committees: standing, select, conference, and joint. **Standing committees** are permanent committees that determine whether proposed legislation should be presented to the entire House or Senate for consideration. The best-known standing committees are Armed Services, Foreign Relations, and Finance in the Senate and National Security, International Relations, Rules, and Ways and Means in the House. Both chambers have committees on agriculture, appropriations, the judiciary, and veterans' affairs. In 1995, the Senate had 16 standing committees, and the House had 19.

Select committees are also known as **special committees.** Unlike standing committees, these are temporary and are established to examine specific issues. They must be reestablished with each new Congress. The purpose of select committees is to investigate matters that have attracted widespread attention, such as illegal immigration or drug use. They do not propose legislation but issue a report at the conclusion of their investigation. If a problem becomes an ongoing concern, Congress may decide to change the status of the committee from select to standing.

Conference committees deal with legislation that has been passed by each of both houses of Congress. The two bills may be similar, but they are seldom identical. The function of the conference committee is to iron out the differences. Members of both the House and Senate who have worked on the bill in their respective standing committees serve on the conference committee. It usually takes just a few days for them to come up with the final wording of the legislation. The bill is then reported out of the conference committee and is voted on by both the House and the Senate.

Like the conference committees, **joint committees** have members from both houses, with the leadership rotating between Senate and House members. They focus on issues of general concern to Congress and investigate problems but do not propose legislation. The Joint Economic Committee, for example, examines the nation's economic policies.

The complexity of lawmaking means that committee work must be divided among **subcommittees,** smaller groups that focus more closely on the issues and draft the bills. The number of subcommittees grew in the 20th century. In 1995, the House had 84 and the Senate had 69 subcommittees. These numbers actually represent a reduction in subcommittees, following an attempt to reform the legislative process. Although subcommittees allow closer focus on issues, they have contributed to the decentralization and fragmentation of the legislative process.

When a House subcommittee is formed, a chair is selected, whose assignment is based on seniority, and a permanent staff is assembled. Then the subcommittee tends to take on a political life of its own. As a result, there are now many legislators who have political influence, while in the past the House was dominated by just a few powerful committee chairs. The increase in subcommittees has also made it possible for interest groups to deal with fewer legislators in pressing their position. It has become more difficult to pass legislation because the sheer number of subcommittees and committees causes deliberations on bills to be more complicated. Once considered an important reform, Congress's decentralized subcommittees have caused unforeseen problems in advancing legislation.

How a Bill Becomes a Law

Each Congress is elected for a two-year term and holds two annual sessions. During that time, as many as 20,000 bills might be introduced, but only 5 to 10 percent of them are actually signed into law. While some may pass through Congress rather quickly, others lead to lengthy hearings in the subcommittees or committees and protracted debates on the floor of the House and Senate. Few legislative proposals emerge from the process exactly as they were first written. What many have called the "dance of legislation" is influenced by partisan politics, the lobbying of interest groups, and public opinion.

A bill is introduced

With the exception of revenue or tax bills, which must originate in the House, legislation can be introduced in either the House or the Senate; sometimes identical bills are introduced in both houses. The majority of bills are written by the executive branch. In the State of the Union address, the president presents a legislative program for the coming session. Members of Congress, usually through their staffs, draft legislation as well. Very often, an interest group that wants a particular law passed will work with congressional staff or the administration to get a bill introduced. A Senate or House member may *sponsor* (introduce) a bill, and the bill may have numerous congressional cosponsors. Each bill is assigned a number (and the prefix HR in the House or S in the Senate) by the clerks of the House or the Senate. Bills are then sent to the appropriate committees by the Speaker of the House or the Senate majority leader.

A bill in committee

A bill goes to one of the standing committees and then to a subcommittee, as determined by the committee chair. The subcommittee holds hearings on the bill, taking testimony from its supporters and opponents. After the hearings, it usually issues a report that is either favorable or unfavorable to the bill. Or it may report out an amended or changed bill or rewrite the original bill entirely as a *committee print.* The standing committee usually accepts the recommendation of its subcommittee.

A bill favorably reported out of a Senate committee is put on the calendar for floor action. The bill's sponsors schedule when the debate on the bill will begin through a **unanimous consent agreement.** The process is different in the House. Here bills must first go through the **Rules Committee,** which decides when the full House will hear the bill, if the bill can be amended from the floor, and how much time will be allowed for debate.

A bill before the full House and Senate

The procedures for debating and voting on legislation are different in the House and the Senate. In the House, each member is allowed five minutes to speak on a bill. If amendments are allowed by the Rules Committee, these must pertain to the bill itself. Amendments are accepted or rejected by a vote of the members present. In the Senate, there is no time limit on debate. A senator who wants to delay action on a bill or kill it altogether may use a tactic called a **filibuster.** This is a marathon speech that may go on for hours with the senator yielding the floor only to members who support his or her position. A filibuster can be cut off only through **cloture.** A petition from a minimum of 16 senators is needed for a cloture vote, and 60 senators must actually vote for cloture to end a filibuster. Even then, each senator can still speak for one hour. The Senate also puts no restrictions on the nature of the amendments to a bill. Amendments completely unrelated to the bill are called **riders.** A senator may add an amendment to a highway bill for a new veterans hospital in his or her state, for example.

Bills are passed in the House and Senate by *voice vote* (either "aye" or "no"), *standing vote* (members must stand up to indicate yes or no), or *roll call vote* (each member's vote for or against a bill is recorded).

Factors influencing voting decisions

Legislators are influenced by a variety of factors in making their voting decisions. The unwritten rules of Congress certainly have a role. Through serving on committees, members develop an expertise in a particular field. Other representatives or senators are likely to accept their judgment that a bill merits their support. They will expect the same deference for a piece of legislation in their area of specialization. Legislators often vote for each other's bills when a bill does not affect their constituency. This is a political technique known as **logrolling.** It is frequently used to advance **pork-barrel legislation**—bills designed to benefit a congressional district or state through the appropriation of federal funds. Highway construction, river and harbor improvements, and military base siting are typical examples of pork-barrel projects.

Party loyalty is probably the most important voting factor. In the 1990s, more than 80 percent of the members of Congress voted according to party affiliation. Interest groups provide information to and put pressure (sometimes subtle, sometimes not) on a legislator to vote one way or another. Industry trade associations, unions, environmental groups, and political action committees employ **lobbyists,** paid professionals who try to influence legislation. The role of these groups is significant because they also contribute money and sometimes volunteers to election campaigns. Also, a call from the president to vote for or against a bill is hard to resist. The president can appeal for the good of the nation or party loyalty, promise to actively support legislation the member of Congress wants, or threaten to cut off campaign funds.

Constituents, the voters that the legislator represents, also exercise considerable influence. A congressperson or senator who consistently votes against what the majority of the "folks back home" wants will soon be out of office. Personal beliefs are certainly a factor in voting decisions. If a member of Congress holds a strong position on an issue, no amount of pressure from party members, lobbyists, the president, or even constituents will make a difference.

The conference committee and action by the president

Similar bills that have been passed independently by the House and the Senate go to a conference committee to resolve the differences. If the committee cannot work out a compromise version, the bill is dead for that session of Congress. The bill that comes out of the committee is sent to both houses for a vote, and it cannot be amended from the floor. If the bill is approved by the House and the Senate, it is sent to the president for final action.

A bill becomes a law when signed by the president. If the president vetoes a bill, Congress can override the veto by a two-thirds vote of both houses. There are many reasons for a president to reject legislation. For example, although the president may be supportive of the bill's main purpose, he may decide that it contains unacceptable riders. If the president does not sign or veto a bill within ten days, the bill becomes law. On the other hand, the bill is dead if Congress adjourns within this ten-day period. This is known as a **pocket veto.** In 1996, Congress gave the president **line-item veto** power, which meant he could reject specific spending items within a larger bill. The U.S. Supreme Court struck down this attempt to increase presidential discretion two years later, however, in a 6-3 opinion written by Justice John Paul Stevens.

Chapter Checkout

Q&A

1. Legislation that has been passed in different forms by each chamber is reconciled into a single bill by

   a. standing committees
   b. select committees
   c. special committees
   d. conference committees
   e. secret committees

2. All presidential appointments must be approved through the advice and consent of

   a. the Senate
   b. the House of Representatives
   c. the Supreme Court
   d. the Office of Management and Budget
   e. the Vice President

3. True or False: It takes only 41 Senators to stop a bill from passing their chamber.

4. Congress took advantage of one of its implied powers when, in the _____ _____ Act of 1973, it tried to regulate when the President could send U.S. troops into combat on foreign soil.

5. The U.S. states of the Southwest and West have gained representatives, and those of the Northeast and Midwest lost them, through the process called _____ that followed the last few federal censuses.

Answers: 1. d **2.** a **3.** T (cloture vote on filibuster) **4.** War Powers **5.** reapportionment

Chapter 4

THE PRESIDENT

Chapter Check-In

❏ Distinguishing the president's formal and informal powers

❏ Recognizing the president's formal and informal duties

❏ Considering the president's role in the larger executive branch

The Constitution established an executive branch headed by a president, which represented a significant departure from the Articles of Confederation. Many of the Founders wanted an even stronger executive, essentially an elected king. However, they realized that memories of the revolution against the British monarch were too fresh to permit such a proposal.

Instead, the Constitution granted the president the power to execute the law and titled the office "Commander in Chief," without specifying exactly what role that person would play in either domestic or foreign policy. People who preferred a weak president could see the position described in the Constitution as nothing more than a **chief clerk,** someone who would carry out the legislative branch's orders but play little political role. But nothing in the language of the Constitution prevented the presidency from developing into more of a **leadership** position, a rival political force to Congress.

Of course, numerous limits were placed on the presidency. Congress may override presidential vetoes. The Senate must approve presidential appointments. The president serves only a four-year term and has been limited to two terms since the Twenty-second Amendment won approval in 1951. As the nation witnessed with President Bill Clinton, a president also may be **impeached**—that is, brought up on formal charges—by the House of Representatives and removed from office if convicted in the Senate. None of these limits has been sufficient, however, to prevent the powers and role of the president from expanding dramatically over the last two centuries.

The Powers of the President

In contrast to the many powers it gives Congress, the Constitution grants few specific powers to the president. Indeed, most of Article II, which deals with the executive branch, relates to the method of election, term and qualifications for office, and procedures for succession and impeachment rather than what the president can do. The powers of the president are not limited to those granted in the Constitution. Presidential authority has expanded through the concept of *inherent powers* (see the section on inherent powers later in this chapter) as well as through legislative action.

Treaty power

The president has the authority to negotiate treaties with other nations. These formal international agreements do not go into effect, however, until ratified by a two-thirds vote of the Senate. Although most treaties are routinely approved, the Senate rejected the Treaty of Versailles (1919), which ended World War I and which President Woodrow Wilson had signed, and, more recently, refused to take action on President Jimmy Carter's SALT II Treaty on arms limitation (1979).

Appointment power

The president selects many people to serve the government in a wide range of offices: most important among them are ambassadors, members of the Supreme Court and the federal courts, and cabinet secretaries. More than 2,000 of these positions require **confirmation** (approval) by the Senate under the "advice and consent" provision of the Constitution. Confirmation hearings can become controversial, as did the hearing for Clarence Thomas, President George Bush's nominee for the Supreme Court. Sometimes appointments to ambassadorships are given as a reward for faithful service to the president's political party or for significant campaign contributions. Such appointments are considered **patronage.**

Legislative powers

The president is authorized to proposed legislation. A president usually outlines the administration's legislative agenda in the *State of the Union address* given to a joint session of Congress each January. The president's veto power is an important check on Congress. If the president rejects a bill, it takes a two-thirds vote of both houses, which is difficult to achieve, to accomplish a veto override.

Other specific powers

The president can call Congress into special session and can adjourn Congress if the House and the Senate cannot agree on a final date. The power to grant pardons for federal crimes (except impeachment) is also given to the president. President Gerald Ford pardoned former President Richard Nixon for any crimes he may have committed while in office, and he was able to do so because Nixon resigned before impeachment charges were brought.

Inherent powers

Inherent powers are those that can be inferred from the Constitution. Based on the major role the Constitution gives the president in foreign policy (that is, the authority to negotiate treaties and to appoint and receive ambassadors), President George Washington declared that the United States would remain neutral in the 1793 war between France and Great Britain. To conduct foreign policy, presidents also have signed **executive agreements** with other countries that do not require Senate action. The Supreme Court ruled that these agreements are within the inherent powers of the president.

As commander in chief of the armed forces, presidents have sent American troops into combat or combat situations without congressional authorization. The experience of the Vietnam War led to the War Powers Act (1973), which requires the president to consult Congress and to withdraw troops after 60 days unless Congress specifically approves their continued deployment. Inherent powers allow a president to respond to a crisis—for example, Abraham Lincoln to the Civil War and Franklin D. Roosevelt to the Depression and World War II—but presidential actions based on them can be limited by legislation or declared unconstitutional by the Supreme Court.

Delegation of powers

Congress has given power to the executive branch in the area of domestic policy. President Roosevelt asked for and received extraordinary authority to do what he thought was necessary to bring the country out of the Depression. Congress has created new cabinet departments and federal agencies that have given the president and the executive branch broad powers to address problems such as education, welfare, and the environment. The trend throughout the 20th century has been to increase presidential powers at the expense of Congress.

The Functions of the President

The president is expected to perform a number of duties as part of the office. While the Constitution mentions several of these duties, others have evolved over time. How presidents carry out these functions depends on their personality, as well as their view of the presidency and the role of government. For example, the State of the Union was not delivered as a speech until the presidency of Woodrow Wilson.

Modern presidents usually take a leadership approach to their job. They consider themselves representatives of all the people, put in place to pursue a political agenda by using their inherent powers. Scholars usually praise presidents who follow this model, because it results in ambitious policy programs that (for good or ill) leave a strong mark on American government. Of course, when presidents view themselves as policymakers, they sometimes are impatient with constitutional limitations on executive activity. For example, Abraham Lincoln suspended the right of *habeas corpus* during the Civil War. Both Andrew Jackson and Franklin Roosevelt tried to intimidate the Supreme Court, some say successfully, after a majority of justices ruled against them.

"Chief clerk" presidents, on the other hand, take a more passive approach to the job. They are much more careful about exceeding their constitutional authority and often believe in a limited government. However, many scholars feel that clerkship presidents such as James Buchanan and Herbert Hoover did not move aggressively enough to deal with crises during their administrations.

Presidents also differ on their conception of the role of the federal government. Lyndon Johnson believed the government had a responsibility to help the disadvantaged. His **Great Society,** the domestic program that included the "War on Poverty" and Medicare, reflected this concern. Ronald Reagan, on the other hand, saw government as the problem, not the solution to the nation's problems.

Commander in chief

The president is the highest-ranking officer in the armed services. As noted previously, presidents have shown no hesitation in filling this role by sending American forces to trouble spots around the world as an instrument of foreign policy. U.S. troops in Grenada, Panama, the Persian Gulf, Haiti, and Bosnia are recent cases in point.

Chief of state

Acting as chief of state is a president's most visible function, whether meeting the heads of other countries, welcoming astronauts or college football champions to the White House, or opening the Olympic Games. Although largely ceremonial, the role of chief of state makes an important statement to the world and the nation about the president as a leader.

Diplomat

The president not only decides the direction of American foreign policy but also plays an important role in carrying it out. During the Cold War era, for example, face-to-face meetings between President Bush and leaders of the Soviet Union contributed to an easing of tensions and important arms control breakthroughs. President Jimmy Carter personally worked out the Camp David Accords between Israel and Egypt. This kind of activity is sometimes called *summit diplomacy.*

Chief executive

The president is the chief administrator, or chief bureaucrat, of the nation and is ultimately responsible for all the programs in the executive branch. Responsible for seeing that "all laws are faithfully executed," a president sets the broad policy for the executive departments and agencies rather than managing their day-to-day operations.

Legislator

A president does not simply propose legislation but is actively involved in seeing that it becomes law. The White House staff maintains close contacts with Congress, while the president meets with Congressional leaders to press for passage of bills and calls individual Congressional members to ask for their vote. In instances of a **divided government,** in which the White House and Congress are controlled by different political parties, the president can appeal directly to the people for support.

Moral leader

The president is expected to set the moral tone for the nation, including exemplary honesty, religious faith, and integrity. The question of a president's moral leadership has assumed new importance in recent years as the media and public have given the private lives of the elected officials closer scrutiny. The "character issue" is frequently included in public opinion polls on a president's performance.

Party leader

In addition to performing clearly governmental functions, the president serves as the "titular head" of a political party. A president is expected to support the party's platform, help raise money for the party, and campaign for the party's candidates. The president expects the support of party members in Congress on key votes; however, recent experience has shown that party loyalty is declining.

A potential conflict exists between the president as national leader and as party leader. Astute presidents address their party's positions realistically while trying to build consensus on nonpartisan issues. The rise of interest groups that take stands on controversial or emotional issues such as abortion, school prayer, and welfare spending can make this balance difficult to achieve.

Organization of the Executive Branch

Policy is not developed nor are all executive decisions made by the president alone. Presidents have come to rely on a large staff based in the White House to handle a wide range of administrative tasks from policymaking to speechwriting. The staff is loyal to the president, not to Congress or a government agency. Unchecked by the president, the White House staff can become a source of scandal. Watergate under President Nixon is a good example.

The Constitution gives practically no direction on the organization of the executive branch. It does mention "executive departments," which became the basis for the cabinet. While relying primarily on the White House staff for advice, a president turns to members of the cabinet for advice in their areas of expertise. In the main, however, cabinet secretaries are responsible for running the departments they head.

The Executive Office of the President

The Executive Office comprises four agencies that advise the president in key policy areas: the White House Office, the National Security Council, the Council of Economic Advisors, and the Office of Management and Budget.

The president's main advisers, often long-time personal friends or people who played a key role in the election, make up the **White House Office.** It includes the president's personal lawyer, press secretary, appointments secretary, and other support personnel. The most important position in this group is the **chief of staff,** who is responsible for seeing that the president's legislative goals are carried out by working with Congress on the legislative agenda.

The National Security Council (NSC), organized in 1947, deals with domestic, foreign, and military policies affecting security issues. By law, the NSC is composed of the president, vice president, secretary of defense, and secretary of state. Representatives of the intelligence and defense communities are also members. The president's national security advisor supervises the council's activities.

The Council of Economic Advisors (CEA) was created in 1946 to provide the president with information on economic policy. It is best known for predicting national economic trends.

The enormously complex task of preparing the federal budget for submission to Congress falls to the Office of Management and Budget (OMB). Originally established in the Treasury Department as the Bureau of the Budget, the OMB has had its powers expanded considerably since 1970. It is involved in drafting the president's legislative program and evaluating how effectively federal agencies use their appropriations.

The cabinet

George Washington appointed the first executive department heads in 1789. They were the attorney general, secretary of state, secretary of treasury, and secretary of war. As the scope and functions of the federal government grew, the number of executive departments increased. The heads of these departments, who all have the title *secretary* (except the *attorney general* of the U.S. Department of Justice), make up the core of the president's **cabinet.** From time to time, the cabinet departments have been reorganized, along with the agencies under them. For example, the Immigration and Naturalization Service (INS) was originally part of the Department of Labor but was transferred to the Justice Department in 1940. The Department of Health, Education, and Welfare (1953) was renamed Health and Human Services in 1979 when a separate Department of Education was established. In addition to the secretaries of the departments, the U.S. ambassador to the United Nations, the OMB director, and other officials participate in the cabinet. Table 4-1 lists the cabinet departments as they have existed since 1989.

Table 4-1   Cabinet Departments (1989)

Justice (1789)	Defense (1947)
State (1789)	Health and Human Services (1953)
Treasury (1789)	Housing and Urban Development (1965)
Interior (1849)	Transportation (1967)
Agriculture (1889)	Energy (1977)
Commerce (1903; originally included Labor)	Education (1979)
Labor (1913)	Veterans Affairs (1989)

In recent years, the cabinet departments have become targets for people who believe that too much power is in the hands of the federal government. For example, some have called for the elimination of the Department of Education, based on the belief that educational policy is best set at the state or local level. Abolishing the Department of Commerce has also been considered.

Unlike the White House staff positions or ambassadorships, cabinet appointments are not usually based on a personal relationship with the president or given as a reward. A president is more likely to base the selections on reputation, expertise, and ability to manage a large bureaucracy. Appointments are also an opportunity for a president to show that the administration represents a broad cross-section of the country by including ethnic and racial minorities and women in the cabinet.

The Vice President and Presidential Succession

Under the Constitution, the vice president serves as the president of the Senate (voting only to break ties) and succeeds the president in the event of death, resignation, or the inability of the president to discharge duties. The process of presidential succession was changed through the Twenty-fifth Amendment, which was a response to the transition following the assassination of President John F. Kennedy in 1963. The orderly transition of power in the executive branch is one of the hallmarks of U.S. constitutional government.

The selection of the vice president

Although the vice president is only "a heartbeat away from the presidency," politics influences this individual's selection more than any qualifications to hold the highest office. President Kennedy chose Lyndon Johnson as his running mate primarily because Johnson was a Southerner who could help carry the key state of Texas; that Johnson was the powerful majority leader of the Senate was less important. Walter Mondale's background in the Senate, on the other hand, made him a logical vice president for Jimmy Carter, who was the governor of Georgia and running as a Washington outsider.

The role of the vice president

Because of a limited constitutionally defined function, the role that a vice president plays is determined by the president. While Harry Truman was vice president, he was kept in the dark about many key issues. He did not learn about the atomic bomb, for example, until after he became president following the death of Franklin Roosevelt. Since 1960, however, the responsibilities of the vice president have expanded. Lyndon Johnson led the nation's space program under Kennedy. Vice President Al Gore was heavily involved in the Clinton administration's policies, especially in areas such as foreign policy, the environment, and streamlining government. Vice President Richard Cheney played a particularly influential role in the transition of President George W. Bush.

The process of presidential succession

Following the assassination of John F. Kennedy, Lyndon Johnson served for a year without a vice president. Under the Twenty-fifth Amendment (1967), the president nominates a vice president, who is confirmed by a majority of both houses of Congress. This process was followed twice in the 1970s, when Gerald Ford became vice president after Spiro Agnew resigned and when Ford appointed Nelson Rockefeller as his vice president after President Nixon resigned. The amendment also provides for the temporary transfer of power to the vice president if the president is incapacitated. In the event that the offices of both president and vice president are vacant simultaneously, the order of succession is the Speaker of the House of Representatives, the president pro tempore of the Senate, the secretary of state, the secretary of defense, and the other cabinet departments.

Chapter Checkout

Q&A

1. Overriding a presidential veto requires a _____ fraction of the vote in each chamber of the Congress.

2. Why do presidents often use executive agreements rather than treaties when negotiating with foreign powers?

    a. Executive agreements don't require the assistance of the Department of State; treaties do.

    b. Executive agreements don't require Senate approval; treaties do.

    c. Executive agreements can be issued in secret; treaties must be publicized.

    d. Foreign powers have more confidence in America's executive agreements.

3. List the four agencies that make up the president's executive office.

Answers: 1. two-thirds **2.** b **3.** NSC, CEA, OMB, WHO

Chapter 5

THE JUDICIARY

Chapter Check-In

❏ Laying out the structure of state and federal courts

❏ Understanding judicial processes at the federal level

❏ Reviewing the most important Supreme Court rulings

The United States has two court systems: 1) the Supreme Court and the lower federal courts, established in somewhat vague terms by Article III of the Constitution, and 2) the state courts. The two systems are somewhat parallel. Ultimately, the federal courts may receive appeals from the state courts, and the Supreme Court has final jurisdiction on constitutional questions.

The State Court System

The state court system is organized as a hierarchy and includes superior courts (which act as trial courts) and a state supreme court. Generally, judges in the state courts are elected.

Superior courts

Superior courts usually function at the county level. A judge, who rules on matters of law such as whether a piece of evidence is admissible, and a jury (if the defendant asks for a jury trial) ideally reach a decision on a case based on the evidence presented. Superior courts handle two types of cases: criminal cases and civil cases. **Criminal cases** involve nonviolent crimes, such as fraud, and violent crimes, such as murder, armed robbery, and rape. Many criminal cases do not come to trial because the **defendant** (the person charged with a crime) enters into a **plea bargain,** an agreement to plead guilty to a lesser charge in return for a reduced sentence. Prosecutors may agree to a plea bargain, which saves the judicial system time and money, because the original charge may be difficult to prove.

Civil cases are disputes over property, money, contracts, or personal well-being (malpractice, libel, and personal injury lawsuits). The **plaintiff** (the person or persons bringing the suit) usually seeks **compensatory damages,** which is money in return for the loss or harm done, and **punitive damages,** which is a monetary award to make it clear to the defendant not to engage in such actions in the future. Punitive damages may exceed the actual harm caused by a person or company many times over, because juries sometimes treat the legal battle as a popularity contest between plaintiff and defendant—a contest that corporations often lose and individual members of a community often win. Some civil cases are brought as **class-action suits.** These are cases in which a large number of people have been affected, and the compensation award is distributed to all the victims. Class-action suits often involve health and product liability questions; suits against manufacturers of asbestos products, tobacco companies, automobile manufacturers, and insurance companies have attracted national attention. Critics argue that activists have turned to class-action lawsuits as a way to circumvent the proper channels of influence in American government. They are trying to get rid of productsthat they oppose, such as cigarettes and handguns, without having to win political support for these goals.

State appellate courts

If a defendant loses at trial and there are questions over legal procedures or matters of law, the case may be appealed to an appellate court. The case is argued before a panel of judges rather than a jury, and the decision is reached by a majority vote. The appellate court can reverse the original verdict, let the verdict stand, or call for a new trial. Of the millions of cases heard by trial courts throughout the country, only a very small percentage is brought to the appellate courts.

State supreme courts

Whatever the outcome at the appellate court, the case may go to the state supreme court, which is a state's appeals court of last resort. Almost all of these appeals come from defendants. Acting as a group, the state supreme court justices hand down decisions that become the highest law in the state.

The election of state judges

Trial, appellate, and state supreme court judges are usually elected. At the municipal and county levels, the term of office is usually four years. Candidates often run unopposed for trial court positions, and the ballot may read, "Shall Candidate x be elected to the Superior Court, Office No. 6?" Voters choose yes or no. The higher courts have 8- or 12-year terms, the length of which is intended to free judges from political influence.

The Federal Court System

With the exception of the Supreme Court, the Constitution left the organization of the federal court system up to Congress. Congress accomplished this task through the Judiciary Act of 1789, which created the three federal court levels: the district courts, the courts of appeal, and the Supreme Court. In addition, legislative and special courts deal with specific types of cases involving narrow legal issues.

District courts

The 94 federal district courts function as both trial and appellate courts. These courts are assigned specific geographic areas in the nation. As a trial court, they have jurisdiction over such federal crimes as mail fraud, counterfeiting, smuggling, and bank robbery. Federal civil cases may involve water rights, interstate commerce, and environmental controversies. About half of the cases tried in district courts are decided by juries.

District courts also serve as the first federal courts to hear state cases involving constitutional questions. The case of *Gideon v. Wainright,* in which the Supreme Court ruled that even a poor defendant has the right to an attorney, began when Clarence Gideon appealed his conviction in a superior court trial.

Courts of appeal

Decisions of the district courts and rulings by federal administrative agencies can be brought to federal courts of appeal. There are 13 such courts, each covering a geographic area called a **circuit.** Eleven of the circuits take in multistate areas. The U.S. Court of Appeals for the Ninth Circuit, for example, includes eight Western states and Alaska. There is a court in the District of Columbia and one that specializes in patents and contract claims against the federal government. The courts of appeal hand down decisions based on the majority vote of a three-judge panel.

As in the state system, there is a winnowing of cases as the appeals are brought to the next level. Of the approximately 276,000 cases heard by the district courts each year, about 48,500 reach the courts of appeal, and the vast majority is resolved there. The Supreme Court may receive as many as 7,000 requests for review, but it takes under consideration fewer than 100 per year.

Legislative and special courts

Some federal courts deal with technical matters of law or specific areas of jurisprudence. These courts include the U.S. Tax Court, the U.S. Court of Military Appeals, and the U.S. Court of Veterans Appeals. Cases tried in any of these courts can be appealed to the district courts.

The Supreme Court

The Constitution establishes the Supreme Court as the highest court in the federal system, and its decisions are the supreme law of the land. The Court currently consists of nine members, one Chief Justice and eight associate justices. Two types of cases come to the Supreme Court: appeals from the courts of appeal (here the Court is said to have *appellate jurisdiction*) and cases involving *original jurisdiction.* As specified in Article III, Section 2, these cases are disputes involving the states or diplomatic personnel from other countries.

The appointment of federal judges

The president appoints all federal judges, including the justices of the Supreme Court, for a life term. The American Bar Association, the national organization of attorneys, rates candidates for the federal bench on a scale ranging from "exceptionally well qualified" to "not qualified." However, the president is under no obligation to pay any attention to the ratings. Federal judges are confirmed by a majority vote of the Senate, often following hearings before the Senate Judiciary Committee. Federal judges may be impeached and removed from office if found guilty of the charges. Judges in the district courts and courts of appeal are required to live within the geographical boundaries of their courts.

The Supreme Court in Operation

The Constitution implies, but does not specifically state, that the Supreme Court has the power to declare laws unconstitutional, both those enacted by Congress and by the states. The principle, which is known as **judicial review,** was firmly established in the case of *Marbury v. Madison* (1803). The decision, issued by Chief Justice John Marshall, was the first time the court invalidated an act of Congress (part of the Judiciary Act of 1789). Under Marshall, other key cases were decided that strengthened the position of the Supreme Court. In *Fletcher v. Peck* (1810), for example, the sanctity of contracts was upheld and a state law was ruled unconstitutional.

The Supreme Court under Marshall practiced *judicial nationalism;* its decisions favored the federal government at the expense of the states. In *McCulloch v. Maryland* (1819), it broadly defined the elastic clause by ruling that a state could not tax a federal bank, and in *Gibbons v. Ogden* (1824), it declared that a state could not regulate interstate commerce.

The Court has not always supported a larger role for the federal government. It initially found much of President Franklin Roosevelt's New Deal legislation unconstitutional, primarily for violating the economic rights of individuals and companies. Roosevelt responded by trying to increase the size of the Court, which would let him appoint new justices sympathetic to his program. This attempt to "pack" the Court failed, but around that time the Court began ruling in Roosevelt's favor anyway.

The appointment of Supreme Court justices

Because Supreme Court justices serve for life and their decisions have a major impact on American society, their appointments are probably the most important that a president makes. The selection is certainly not above politics. Historically, 90 percent of the justices come from the same political party as the president who appointed them. As with the cabinet, concern about making the Court more inclusive is also a factor. The overriding concern, however, is usually a nominee's *judicial philosophy:* How does a candidate view the role of the Court, and what is his or her stand on the issues that might come before the Court?

Unlike the hearings for judges in the lower federal courts, the confirmation of Supreme Court justices is highly publicized and sometimes controversial. Robert Bork, a conservative nominated by President Ronald Reagan, was rejected by the Democrat-controlled Senate. Clarence Thomas narrowly won confirmation following highly emotional hearings during which charges of sexual harassment were made against him. The attention given the confirmation process reflects the impact that the Court's decisions have on Americans' lives and the issues about which they have strong feelings, such as abortion, school prayer, and the rights of criminal defendants.

A case comes to the Supreme Court

Cases are appealed to the Supreme Court through a **writ of certiorari,** which is a request for review based on the particular issues in the case. The Court may receive as many as 7,000 such appeals during a term. These are screened and summarized by the justices' law clerks, and the summaries are discussed in conferences held twice a week. Under the so-called *rule of four,* only four of the nine justices have to agree to hear a case before it is placed on the **docket.** The *docket* is the Supreme Court's agenda and, in effect, the list of cases accepted for review. Typically, the Court considers only about 100 cases a year; for the remainder, the decision of the lower court stands.

A case before the Court

Attorneys for both sides file *briefs,* which are written arguments that contain the facts and legal issues involved in the appeal. The term is misleading because a "brief" may run hundreds of pages and include sociological, historical, and scientific evidence, as well as legal arguments. Groups or individuals who are not directly involved in the litigation but have an interest in the outcome may submit, with permission of the Court, an **amicus curiae** (literally "friend of the court") **brief** stating their position. After the briefs are filed, attorneys may present their case directly to the Court through oral arguments. Just 30 minutes are allotted to each side, and the attorneys' arguments may be frequently interrupted by questions from the justices.

A decision is reached

After reviewing the briefs and hearing oral arguments, the justices meet in conference to discuss the case and ultimately take a vote. A majority of the justices must agree, meaning five out of the nine justices in a full Court. At this point, the *opinion* is drafted. This is the written version of the Court's decision. If in the majority, the chief justice can draft the opinion, but more often this task is assigned to another justice in the majority. The senior associate justice voting in the majority makes the assignment when the chief justice is in the minority.

The opinion usually goes through numerous drafts, which are circulated among the justices for comment. Additional votes are sometimes required, and a justice may change from one side to another. After final agreement is reached, a **majority opinion** is issued that states the Court's decision (judgment) and presents the reasons behind the decision (argument). Usually the decision builds on previous court rulings, called **precedent,** because a central principle guiding judicial practices is the doctrine of **stare decisis** (which means "let the decision stand"). A justice who accepts the decision but not the majority's reasoning may write a **concurring opinion.** Justices who remain opposed to the decision may submit a **dissenting opinion.** Some dissents have been so powerful that they are better remembered than the majority opinion. It may also happen that, as the times and the makeup of the Court change, a dissenting view becomes the majority opinion in a subsequent case. When the Court chooses to overrule precedent, however, the justices responsible may be criticized for violating the stare decisis principle.

The rationale for decisions

Sometimes Supreme Court decisions require **statutory interpretation,** or the interpretation of federal law. Here the Court may rely on the plain meaning of a law to determine what Congress or a state legislature intended, or it may turn to the legislative history, the written record of how the bill became a law. Similar forms of reasoning apply in cases of **constitutional interpretation,** but justices (especially liberals) often are willing to use a third method: the *living Constitution* approach. They update the meaning of provisions, sticking neither to literal interpretation nor to historical intent, so that the Constitution can operate as "a living document."

Court watchers group the justices into liberal, moderate, and conservative camps. The members of the Court certainly have personal views, and it is naive to believe that these views do not play a part in decisions. What is more important, however, is how a justice views the role of the Court. Proponents of **judicial restraint** see the function of the judiciary as interpreting the law, not making new law, and they tend to follow statutes and precedents closely. Those who support **judicial activism,** on the other hand, interpret legislation more loosely and are less bound by precedent. They see the power of the Court as a means of encouraging social and economic policies.

Implementing Supreme Court decisions

The Supreme Court has no power to enforce its decisions. It cannot call out the troops or compel Congress or the president to obey. The Court relies on the executive and legislative branches to carry out its rulings. In some cases, the Supreme Court has been unable to enforce its rulings. For example, many public schools held classroom prayers long after the Court had banned government-sponsored religious activities.

Table 5-1 lists some of the more important Supreme Court decisions over the years and briefly explains the impact of each decision.

Table 5-1   Important Supreme Court Decisions

Marbury v. Madison (1803): Established the principle of judicial review by declaring part of the Judiciary Act of 1789 unconstitutional.

Fletcher v. Peck (1810): The first case to declare a state law unconstitutional.

McCulloch v. Maryland (1819): A state cannot tax an instrumentality of the federal government.

Trustees of Dartmouth College v. Woodward (1819): Private charters are protected by the Constitution.

Cohens v. Virginia (1821): The federal courts have jurisdiction over state cases involving federal rights.

Gibbons v. Ogden (1824): The federal government has the right to control interstate commerce.

Cherokee Nation v. Georgia (1831): Declared the Cherokee a dependent domestic nation possessing some sovereignty.

Worcester v. Georgia (1832): Georgia has no force in Cherokee territory.

Commonwealth v. Hunt (1842): Workers have the right to organize.

Dred Scott v. Sandford (1857): Slaves were property and remained slaves, even when taken to free territories or states.

Ex Parte Milligan (1866): When federal courts are open during wartime, military courts do not take precedence.

Munn v. Illinios (1877): When private property affects public interest, states can act when federal policy is absent.

Wabash, St. Louis, and Pacific Railroad Co. v. Illinois (1886): Only the federal government can regulate interstate commerce.

U.S. v. E.C. Knight Co. (1895): First case under Sherman Antitrust Act; manufacturing is not the same as commerce.

Plessy v. Ferguson (1896): Established the principle of "separate but equal" between the races (segregation).

Insular Cases (1901, 1903, 1904): The Constitution does not "follow the flag"; Congress must determine the procedural rights of a territory.

Northern Securities Co. v. U.S. (1904): A holding company owning stock of competing railroads violates the Sherman Antitrust Act.

Muller v. Oregon (1908): Upheld women's work hour laws.

Danbury Hatters Case (Lowe v. Lawler) (1908): A union boycott violates the Sherman Antitrust Act.

Schenck v. U.S. (1919): No freedom is absolute; every act must be judged according to circumstances; established Justice Oliver Wendell Holmes, Jr.'s "clear and present danger" test.

Adkins v. Children's Hospital (1923): Denied congressional and state regulation of a minimum wage.

Schechter Poultry Corp. v. U.S. (1935): Declared the National Industrial Recovery Act unconstitutional.

(continued)

Table 5-1 *(continued)*

U.S. v. Butler (1936): Declared the Agricultural Adjustment Act of 1933 unconstitutional.

National Labor Relations Board v. Jones and Laughlin Steel Corp. (1937): Upheld the National Labor Relationis Act.

West Virginia Board of Education v. Barnette (1943): Reversed the Gobitis decision of 1940, which upheld expulsion of some Jehovah's Witnesses children from school for refusal to salute the American flag.

Korematsu v. U.S. (1944): Upheld the arrest and conviction of Fred Korematsu for noncompliance with a military order for those of Japanese ancestry to go to relocation centers.

Brown v. Board of Education of Topeka (1954): Ended the segregation of public schools.

Gideon v. Wainwright (1963): A lawyer must be provided to those charged with a felony, even if they can't pay.

Escobedo v. Illinois (1964): If requested, a lawyer must be present during police interrogation before an indictment is made.

Miranda v. Arizona (1966): Accused individuals have the right to remain silent and must be informed of their rights.

Roe v. Wade (1973): A woman has the right to decide whether to have an abortion.

Chapter Checkout

Q&A

1. Federal courts generally try to base their rulings on previous decisions, called precedents, following a doctrine represented by the Latin term
   a. certiori
   b. amicus curiae
   c. prima facie
   d. stare decisis
   e. caveat emptor
   f. gladius amoris

2. The Constitution does not explicitly give the U.S. Supreme Court the power of _____ _____, which allows it to strike down state and federal laws as unconstitutional.

3. Prosecutors and defendants often negotiate a _____ _____, in which the accused admits to a lesser crime, in order to reduce overload on the legal system.

4. Supreme Court opinions that disagree with both the Court majority's judgment and its reasoning are called _____ opinions, whereas those that disagree only with the reasoning are called _____ opinions.

Answers: 1. d **2.** judicial review **3.** plea bargain **4.** dissenting, concurring

Critical Thinking

1. Justices may use at least three methods when interpreting law: the plain meaning, historical intent, and living Constitution approaches. What are the advantages and disadvantages of each?

Chapter 6

THE BUREAUCRACY

Chapter Check-In

❏ Considering the traits of bureaucratic organizations

❏ Tracking the growth of the federal government

❏ Seeking ways to get the bureaucracy under control

A bureaucracy is a system of organization noted for its size and complexity. Everything within a bureaucracy—responsibilities, jobs, and assignments—exists to achieve some goal. Bureaucracies are found at the federal, state, county, and municipal levels of government, and even large private corporations may be bureaucratically organized. People who work for government agencies, from high-level managers and executives to clerical staff, are called **bureaucrats.** The superintendent of a large urban school district is a bureaucrat, as are the teachers, librarians, nurses, and security guards.

The terms *bureaucrat* and *bureaucracy* have negative connotations. They bring to mind long, difficult forms; standing in long lines; and encounters with inflexible and unsympathetic clerks. The simplest requests are tangled in **red tape,** the paperwork that slows down accomplishment of an otherwise simple task. Despite this popular perception, bureaucracy is necessary for big governmental agencies to operate.

Characteristics of a Bureaucracy

All bureaucracies share similar characteristics, including specialization, hierarchical organization, and formal rules. In the best circumstances, these characteristics allow a bureaucracy to function smoothly.

Specialization

Workers in a bureaucracy perform specialized tasks that call for training and expertise. Trained personnel can accomplish their jobs efficiently. The downside of specialization is that bureaucrats often cannot (or refuse to) "work out of class," that is, take on a task that is outside the scope of their job description.

Hierarchical organization

The structure of a bureaucracy is called a *hierarchy,* a succession of tiers from the most menial worker in the organization to the highest executive. Each level has clearly defined authority and responsibilities.

Formal rules

Bureaucracies function under formal rules. These instructions state how all tasks in the organization, or in a particular tier of the hierarchy, are to be performed. The rules are often called *standard operating procedures* (SOP) and are formalized in procedures manuals. By following the rules, bureaucrats waste no time in making appropriate decisions.

There are contradictions in the operation of a bureaucracy, however. The narrow focus on special expertise may blind a bureaucrat to a flaw in the performance of a task. Compounding the problem may be the bureaucrat's inability to recognize the problem if it occurs in an area outside the bureaucrat's expertise. The hierarchical structure also prevents a democratic approach to problem-solving. Lower-level staff find it difficult to question the decisions of supervisors, and executives and managers may be unaware that a problem exists several rungs down the organizational ladder.

The Growth of the Federal Bureaucracy

The federal bureaucracy began with the three cabinet departments established by George Washington in 1789. Since that time, not only have the number of departments in the cabinet more than tripled, but now there are also myriad agencies, bureaus, government corporations, authorities, and administrations that take care of the government's business.

The nature of the civil service

For the purposes of this book, the **civil service** refers to the civilian employees of the federal government. Wealthy men dominated the bureaucracy through the 1820s. This changed with the election of President Andrew Jackson (1828), who opened government jobs to the common people. He inaugurated the **spoils system,** under which party loyalty—not experience or talent—became the criterion for a federal job. This was the beginning of **patronage,** and it continued through the late 19th century. Congress passed the **Pendleton Act** in 1883, which created a system for hiring federal workers based on qualifications rather than political allegiance; employees were also protected from losing their jobs when the administration changed. To encourage a nonpartisan bureaucracy, the **Hatch Act** (1939) prohibited federal workers from running for office or actively campaigning for other candidates. Such limitations on civil liberties are considered by many the price that has to be paid for a professional, nonpolitical bureaucracy.

The rise of the welfare state

During the 1930s, the size of the federal bureaucracy mushroomed due to President Franklin Roosevelt's New Deal agencies. Although many were short-lived, others continue to play a role in the lives of Americans: the Social Security Administration (SSA), the Securities and Exchange Commission (SEC), the Tennessee Valley Authority (TVA), the Federal Trade Commission (FTC), and the Federal Deposit Insurance Corporation (FDIC). Out of these agencies' programs grew the concept of the **welfare state,** under which the federal government, rather than individuals, municipalities, or the states, assumes the major responsibility for the well-being of the people. President Lyndon Johnson's Great Society during the 1960s expanded the welfare state with such programs as Medicare, Head Start, the Job Corps, and the Office of Economic Opportunity (OEO). As with the New Deal, many Great Society programs became a permanent part of the federal bureaucracy. The idea of the government seeing to the needs of its citizens carried on into the 1970s: The Environmental Protection Agency (EPA) was created by the Nixon administration, the new Occupational Safety and Health Administration (OSHA) in the Labor Department transformed the workplace for most Americans, and new cabinet departments were established (see Chapter 4).

National security bureaucracy

The federal bureaucracy deals with more than social and economic policies. A large number of agencies are responsible for protecting the American people from both foreign and domestic dangers. The national security bureaucracy includes the Federal Bureau of Investigation (FBI), the Central Intelligence Agency (CIA), the National Security Agency (NSA), and the Defense Intelligence Agency (DIA). Responding to late 20th-century public concern about violent crime, drugs, and illegal immigration into the United States, agencies such as the Bureau of Alcohol, Tobacco, and Firearms (ATF), the Drug Enforcement Administration (DEA), and the Immigration and Naturalization Service (INS) have increased in size.

Controlling the Size of Bureaucracy

In the 1980s and 1990s, calls for controlling the federal bureaucracy became commonplace. The public saw the bureaucracy as being too large and lacking in accountability. Bureaucracy can be reduced in a number of ways, although success is often limited.

Appointment power and presidential persuasion

The president appoints the key members of the federal bureaucracy. If committed to controlling the size of government, the president will select people who are determined to streamline and increase the efficiency of the departments or agencies they lead. A president can give ongoing direction by conferring frequently with cabinet secretaries on policy matters and demonstrating a keen interest in their work. Under such influence, an agency may become more innovative and productive.

Reorganization

Since the 1960s, various government agencies have been moved from one cabinet department to another, and the functions of the departments themselves have been redefined. For example, the former Department of Health, Education, and Welfare was split into the Department of Health and Human Services and the Department of Education. A serious question remains, however, whether reorganization really improves governmental efficiency. Bureaucracies take on a life of their own and, once created, are difficult to dismantle. President Ronald Reagan failed in his plans to eliminate, or at least downgrade, the Departments of Energy and Education, and during his term, the Veterans Administration was added to the cabinet.

Privatization and deregulation

Some critics of the size of government argue that certain responsibilities should be turned over to private enterprise, which can carry out programs with less cost and more efficiency. The example frequently cited compares Federal Express to the U.S. Postal Service. Privatization has been most successful when undertaken by local government.

Deregulation means that the federal government reduces its role and allows an industry greater freedom in how it operates. A reduction in the federal government's responsibility certainly affects the size of the bureaucracy. However, the consequences of deregulation may outweigh the benefits, as seen in the savings and loan scandals of the 1980s following deregulation of the savings industry.

The power of the budget

Since 1970, the Office of Management and Budget (OMB) has been charged with preparing the administration's budget. A president can use the OMB to shape agencies and their programs by reducing or enlarging their proposed appropriations. Under Ronald Reagan, major federal regulations were sent to the OMB for review. Congress's "power of the purse" gives it important oversight authority over the federal bureaucracy. Through the appropriations process, Congress can eliminate a program completely by denying it funds, use the threat of funding cutbacks to control it, or pass new laws that limit the scope of an agency's responsibilities.

Sunset laws

Many states have adopted *sunset laws* requiring periodic cost-effectiveness and efficiency reviews of programs and the agencies that implement them. Those that fail to meet the standards are abolished or reorganized. It takes considerable political will to pass such laws, and that hasn't happened at the federal level.

Executive branch reviews of the federal bureaucracy

Both Presidents George Bush and Bill Clinton attempted to come to grips with the federal bureaucracy through close review of its operation. Under Bush, Vice President Dan Quayle headed the Council on Competitiveness to examine all federal regulations. Vice President Al Gore's report on the six-month national performance review requested by President Clinton (titled *From Red Tape to Results: Creating a Government that Works Better and Costs Less*) called for downsizing some agencies, reorganizing others, and simplifying procedures. Often such proposals run into opposition from the bureaucrats themselves and from the members of Congress who would have to accomplish the proposals' aims. An entrenched bureaucracy has little incentive to decrease its size despite the fact that the public may want reform, and politicians find reducing the size of the federal government an easy campaign issue. Whether the bureaucracy can be moved in the direction the people or president want depends to a large degree on its willingness to be moved.

The Functions of the Federal Bureaucracy

The federal bureaucracy performs three primary tasks in government: implementation, administration, and regulation.

When Congress passes a law, it sets down guidelines to carry out the new policies. Actually putting these policies into practice is known as **implementation.** Often, policy directives are not clearly defined, and bureaucrats must interpret the meaning of the law. The bureaucracy often has some flexibility, known as *administrative discretion,* in actual implementation.

The routine of bureaucracy—collecting fees, issuing permits, giving tests, and so on—is the *administration* of its defined purpose.

The federal bureaucracy makes **regulations** (the rules by which federal and state programs operate) through an administrative process known as *rule making*. Regulations can be challenged in court, and they are not put into effect until the legal issues are resolved.

The Structure of the Federal Bureaucracy

The bureaucracy that implements, administers, and regulates federal programs is in the executive branch. However, Congress and the courts have bureaucracies of their own. Each member of Congress, for example, has a staff that manages the office and helps draft legislation. Congressional committees also have their own staffs, as do the Congressional Budget Office (CBO) and the Office of Technology Assessment (OTA). (Congress created the latter in the 1970s.) These two offices provide in-depth analysis of the operations of federal agencies. The following sections focus only on the executive branch bureaucracies.

Cabinet departments

The **cabinet departments,** the largest administrative units in the federal bureaucracy, have responsibility for broad areas of government operations such as foreign policy (Department of State) and law enforcement (Department of Justice). The departments are organized hierarchically and include bureaus, divisions, offices, and agencies. The FBI, for example, is a bureau of the Justice Department and has 58 field offices throughout the country.

Independent agencies

Independent agencies are created by Congress and do not operate within the cabinet structure. The most important agencies include the CIA, the National Aeronautics and Space Administration (NASA), and the Small Business Administration (SBA). Independent agencies are often created by presidential direction; President John F. Kennedy's Peace Corps is an example. **Regulatory commissions** are also independent of cabinet departments. Many are run by boards whose members are appointed by the president for limited terms. They deal with such matters as product safety and economic policy and include such agencies as the Federal Communications Commission (FCC), the Federal Trade Commission (FTC), the Federal Energy Regulatory Commission (FERC), the Federal Reserve Board, and the SEC.

Government corporations

While often run like private businesses, **government corporations** may receive all or part of their operating capital from appropriations and are run by boards appointed by the president. The TVA, for example, provides electricity, operates recreational facilities, and manages flood control projects in large parts of the Southeastern United States. Much of its income comes from the sale of electricity. On the other hand, the Corporation for Public Broadcasting (CPB) relies heavily on congressional funding to supplement the contributions collected by affiliate radio and television stations during their fund drives. Other government corporations include the FDIC and the Export-Import Bank.

Chapter Checkout

Q&A

1. Scandals swept the savings and loan industry in the late 1980s soon after government applied a policy of
   a. deregulation
   b. privatization
   c. triangulation
   d. capitalization
   e. paralyzation

2. Most government workers in the 19th century received their jobs through political patronage, but this practice has diminished, a process started by the _____ Act of 1883.

3. Drawing from what you have read in this chapter, list five ways the President can try to get the federal bureaucracy under control.

Answers: 1. a **2.** Pendleton **3.** (a) appoint people committed to the president's policies, (b) monitor agency actions, (c) reorganize to increase efficiency, (d) privatize government functions, (e) deregulate industries watched by government

Chapter 7
PUBLIC OPINION

Chapter Check-In

❑ Understanding how pollsters measure opinion

❑ Exploring the sources of public opinion

❑ Tracing the connection between opinion and ideologies

Public opinion refers to attitudes and positions that the American people hold on particular issues facing the country. It is often sharply divided on emotional issues such as affirmative action or gay rights. Opinion on a particular issue usually changes only gradually, if at all. For example, the distribution of opinion on abortion has hardly moved since the early 1970s.

In the rare case when public opinion shifts sharply on an issue, research shows that policy often follows suit. However, the public certainly does not always get its way on policies. Sometimes the reason is that certain groups in the populace are particularly committed and intense in their beliefs. A good example is gun control; a large majority of Americans want more of it, but those who oppose it feel much more strongly and are willing to work much harder to achieve their political goals. Another barrier to popular passions is the Supreme Court. For example, although large majorities of Americans prefer laws allowing prayer in schools or banning flag burning, even relatively conservative Supreme Courts have ruled that government would violate the constitutional rights of minorities if it created either policy.

How Public Opinion Is Measured

Accurate measurement of public opinion through polls is a relatively recent phenomenon. George Gallup and Elmo Roper first developed statistical techniques for this purpose in the 1930s, but many refinements to their methods have been necessary. For example, Gallup had to change how interviewees were selected after predicting that Thomas Dewey would defeat Harry Truman in 1948. Fortunately, polling organizations learn from experience.

Polling techniques

Television stations often ask viewers to call so that they may express an opinion for or against a particular policy. Newspapers and Internet sites also occasionally indulge in this form of entertainment. These gimmicks may be called "polls," but they are completely unscientific because respondents choose whether to participate, and the group that is motivated enough to do so will not represent everyone else in a community. A key element of *scientific* polling, by contrast, is the **representative sample,** which requires that every possible respondent has the same probability of participating. This is accomplished today by using computers to dial telephone numbers randomly and then picking which person in a household to interview using another random method.

Obviously, no poll is perfect. But if the pollster succeeds at generating a random sample, then between 1,200 and 1,500 people will give an accurate picture of national opinion. The level of accuracy is often called the **margin of error** and indicates how much answers will bounce around the truth from poll to poll. Some people wrongly assume that the margin must include the truth, so if a poll estimates that 54 percent of Americans oppose the licensing of gun owners, with a margin of 3 percentage points, they assume the truth must lie between 51 percent and 57 percent. This is not true, however. One time in 20 a poll will draw an unlucky sample, one that represents national opinion poorly, even if the pollster did everything right.

Avoiding bias

In addition to sampling errors, polls can be biased by the type of questions asked and the way the polls are conducted. Questions must be as neutral as possible to avoid skewed results. "Do you believe serial murderers should be executed?" gets a much different response from "Do you support capital punishment?" Interviewers must be careful not to inject their own views into the process by how they ask a question. A poll is also only as good as the respondents, and its validity clearly depends on their willingness to tell the truth about their positions.

Polls are an integral part of American politics. Besides the polling organizations, the news media routinely conduct and report the results of their own surveys. Pollsters also have high-profile positions on campaign and White House staffs. This concern for measuring public opinion indicates that public opinion is useful in understanding the positions of the American people and what policies they support.

Political Socialization

Political socialization is a lifelong process by which people form their ideas about politics and acquire political values. The family, educational system, peer groups, and the mass media all play a role. While family and school are important early in life, what our peers think and what we read in the newspaper and see on television have more influence on our political attitudes as adults.

Family

Our first political ideas are shaped within the family. Parents seldom "talk politics" with their young children directly, but casual remarks made around the dinner table or while helping with homework can have an impact. Family tradition is particularly a factor in party identification, as indicated by the phrases "lifelong Republican" and "lifelong Democrat." The family may be losing its power as an agent of socialization, however, as institutions take over more of child care and parents perform less of it.

Schools

Children are introduced to elections and voting when they choose class officers, and the more sophisticated elections in high school and college teach the rudiments of campaigning. Political facts are learned through courses in American history and government, and schools, at their best, encourage students to critically examine government institutions. Schools themselves are involved in politics; issues such as curriculum reform, funding, and government support for private schools often spark a debate that involves students, teachers, parents, and the larger community.

Peer groups

Although peer pressure certainly affects teenagers' lifestyles, it is less evident in developing their political values. Exceptions are issues that directly affect them, such as the Vietnam War during the 1960s. Later, if peers are defined in terms of occupation, then the group does exert an influence on how its members think politically. For example, professionals such as teachers or bankers often have similar political opinions, particularly on matters related to their careers.

Mass media

Much of our political information comes from the mass media: newspapers, magazines, radio, and television. The amount of time the average American family watches TV makes it the dominant information source.

TV not only helps shape public opinion by providing news and analysis, but also its entertainment programming addresses important contemporary issues that are in the political arena, such as drug use, abortion, and crime.

Social Background and Political Values

The position an individual takes on an issue often reflects his or her place in society. Studies that identify interviewees by income and education, religion, race or ethnicity, region, and gender show that people who have the same social background usually share the same political ideas.

Income and education

Low-income Americans tend to endorse a stronger economic role for the federal government than do wealthier Americans, particularly by supporting programs such as welfare and increases in the minimum wage. This difference is to be expected because wealthier Americans are the ones who mostly pay for such programs, and they naturally want to hold down their tax burden. Nevertheless, even low-income Americans are less likely to consider redistribution of wealth a valid governmental task than are adults socialized in other industrialized countries (such as European nations). Americans generally favor a limited government and emphasize the ability of everyone to succeed through hard work. This belief in individual responsibility may overcome a worker's self-interest in endorsing large social programs.

Race and ethnicity

Polls taken before and after the verdict in the O.J. Simpson criminal trial showed that an overwhelming majority of African Americans believed that the former football star was innocent, while whites felt he was guilty by a similar majority. These results reflect deep differences between the two groups in their perceptions of the judicial system and the role of the police in society.

Self-interest also plays a significant role in attitudes on racial policies. Racial and ethnic minorities tend to favor **affirmative action** programs, designed to equalize income, education, professional opportunity, and the receipt of government contracts. Because such policies make it easier for members of minority groups, such as African Americans and Hispanics, to get good jobs and become affluent, group members naturally support them at a high rate. Supporters defend affirmative action as a way to eliminate ongoing racial discrimination, make up for historical discrimination, and/or increase diversity in businesses and institutions. Americans of European, Asian, or Middle Eastern descent, by contrast, are much more likely to see such programs as reverse discrimination that punishes them for their ethnic backgrounds. A similar pattern is seen in political party affiliation. Beginning with the presidency of Franklin Roosevelt, African Americans switched their allegiance from the Republicans, the "party of Lincoln," to the Democrats.

Religion

The concept of the separation of church and state does not prevent religion from acting as a force in American politics. Strongly held beliefs affect the stand individuals take on issues such as public school prayer and state aid to private or parochial schools. Religion can also determine attitudes on abortion and gay and lesbian rights, irrespective of other factors. It is important to recognize, however, that the major religious groups in the United States—Protestant, Catholic, and Jewish as well as the growing Islamic—have their own liberal and conservative wings that frequently oppose each other on political issues.

Region

The region of the country a person lives in can affect political attitudes. The Southern states tend to support a strong defense policy, a preference reinforced by the presence of many military installations in the region. The South's traditional conservatism was recognized in Richard Nixon's so-called **Southern strategy,** which began the process of strengthening the Republican party in the region. Moreover, issues that are vital in one particular region generate little interest in others—agricultural price supports in the Midwest or water rights and access to public lands in the West, for example. Questions about Social Security and Medicare have an added importance in the Sunbelt states with their high percentage of older adults.

Gender

Gender gap, a term that refers to the varying political opinions men and women hold, is a recent addition to the American political lexicon. Unmarried women hold political views distinct from those of men and married women, views that lead them to support the Democratic party at a disproportionate rate. Studies indicate that more women than men approve of gun control, want stronger environmental laws, oppose the death penalty, and support spending on social programs. These "compassion" issues are usually identified with the Democratic party. It is interesting to note that on abortion, there is very little difference between men's and women's opinions.

Events may also have a place in how people look at politics. In the last 35 years, the country has experienced a divisive war, widespread fraud in the banking and securities industries, and scandals such as Watergate, Iran-Contra, and President Bill Clinton's impeachment. An unusually high number of members of the House and Senate decided not to run for reelection in the early 1990s because they were frustrated with *gridlock* in Congress (the inability to move legislation through). There is a perception that these developments turned people off to politics. Although voter turnout for the presidential elections has been declining over a long period, it showed a healthy jump in 1992, apparently because Ross Perot's independent presidential bid turned out many Americans who otherwise do not vote for major-party candidates. Other measures of political participation, such as following and working for a campaign, have remained relatively stable.

Political Ideology

A *political ideology* is a coherent set of views on politics and the role of the government. Consistency over a wide range of issues is the hallmark of a political ideology. However, given the often contradictory variables that go into molding public opinion and political values (outlined in the previous sections), there is reason to question whether Americans think in ideological terms at all. The exceptions would be the activists in political parties or in groups that espouse specific causes.

In contrast to other countries, Americans have shown essentially no interest in political ideologies either on the extreme left (communism) or the extreme right (fascism). American politics functions largely in the middle of the political spectrum as a contest between liberals and conservatives.

Liberals

Classic liberalism held to the doctrine of **laissez-faire,** which holds that the government should be small and keep out of most areas of American life (such as the economy, community life, and personal morality). What is called liberalism today is quite different. Liberals believe government has an important place both as a regulator in the public interest and to assist those with lower incomes. On the other hand, they still oppose government intervention in matters of personal autonomy. Only **libertarians** still espouse classical liberalism, but Americans holding this political ideology are scattered across various political parties, including the Republicans, the Democrats, and various third parties such as the Libertarian, Reform, and Green parties.

Conservatives

Conservatives feel there is too much government interference, particularly at the federal level, in the economy. This belief translates into calls for lower taxes, reduced spending on social programs, and deregulation. However, many conservatives welcome government support to further their moral agenda. Liberals and conservatives also take opposing positions on crime, with the former concerned with the underlying socioeconomic causes and the latter focusing on the deterrent effect of punishment.

Moderates

Perhaps because most Americans see themselves as moderates, politicians find it difficult to stay within the ideological boundaries of liberalism or conservatism. Many stress their credentials as fiscal conservatives while taking liberal positions on social issues. Others take a **populist** line, embracing active governmental intervention in both economic and cultural spheres. Pat Buchanan, who has run for president under both Republican and Reform labels, usually offers populist appeals. Alabama Governor George Wallace, a presidential candidate in the 1960s, also usually endorsed populist positions.

How Public Opinion Is Formed

Americans have a tremendous amount of information about politics available to them. The mass media, television and its expanding cable and satellite outlets in particular, provide a daily stream of news and analysis. During an election year, the stream becomes a torrent. The availability of information does not necessarily mean that it is absorbed and used, however. Americans may be politically engaged, but research shows that many are unfamiliar with how their government works and what candidates stand for, and many are ignorant about the basic facts of public policy. This lack of knowledge does not prevent Americans from expressing their opinions. Rarely does someone say, "I can't comment on that; I don't have enough information." How then is public opinion formed?

Personal interest

Personal interest has a straightforward effect on public opinion. Individuals respond to a problem based on how the outcome will affect them. This is rather obvious on pocketbook issues: cutting the capital gains tax or increasing co-payments under Medicare can have an immediate and direct impact on people's lives. Self-interest does not apply to all areas of political debate. Whether or not the United States sends troops to Bosnia, for example, is not relevant on a personal level to most Americans unless they are in the armed services or have a family member who is.

Schemas

A more encompassing way of looking at public opinion is through the concept of a *schema,* a term political scientists have borrowed from psychology. A **schema** is a set of beliefs that people use to examine a specific subject. It is a mature outlook that draws on life experiences and, in a sense, is the sum total of the influences of socialization, background, and ideological convictions. Political affiliation is an example of a schema. People who identify themselves as Roosevelt Democrats tend to support a large role for government in society and favor legislation to assist the poor. Free-market Republicans, on the other hand, tend to view government interference in commerce as a dangerous loss of freedom, one that distorts markets and therefore makes society poorer by reducing economic efficiency.

Effective leadership

Politicians are often accused of following the polls too closely, altering their positions to reflect shifts in public opinion. Effective leaders, in contrast, help build a consensus on policies that they believe are in the best interest of the country. The role as an opinion-maker is almost always assumed by the president. George Bush, for example, was not very successful with his economic policy, especially when compared to Ronald Reagan; however, he did an excellent job capturing both American and international public opinion following the Iraqi invasion of Kuwait in 1990.

Chapter Checkout

Q&A

1. Why is the family losing influence as an agent of political socialization?

   a. Young people tend to be Democrats and older people Republicans.

   b. Women tend to be Democrats but men tend to be Republicans.

   c. A concern for "family values" has led relatives to stop discussing controversial subjects.

   d. Institutions have taken increasing responsibility for child care.

2. Which ideology usually opposes an active federal government in both economic and cultural spheres of life?

   a. classical liberalism or libertarianism (associated with various third parties)

   b. modern liberalism (associated with the Democratic party)

   c. modern conservatism (associated with the Republican party)

   d. populism (associated with Pat Buchanan and George Wallace)

   e. journalism (associated with news analysts who think politicians should stop pandering to voters)

3. True or False: Religion plays little role in American politics because the United States has a strong belief in the separation of church and state.

4. True or False: You read that, according to a Roper poll, 63 percent of Americans approve of the job George W. Bush is doing as president, with a margin of error of +/– 3 percent. This means you can be certain that between 60 percent and 66 percent of Americans approve of Bush's performance.

Answers: 1. d **2.** a **3.** F **4.** F (one in 20 chance the margin will miss the truth)

Critical Thinking

1. Many Americans choose their political opinions based upon self-interest. On balance, do you think using political activity to promote one's own interests is a healthy or an unhealthy tendency in the political system?

Chapter 8

THE MASS MEDIA

Chapter Check-In

❑ Tracing the mass media's history

❑ Understanding the environment in which media operate

❑ Reviewing the roles played by journalists

Mass media organizations are not part of the American political structure. Voters do not elect journalists, nor do journalists hold any formal powers or privileges (aside from those stemming from the First Amendment right to a free press). Research also shows that the mass media do not exercise direct influence over people, either officials or regular voters. Neither endorsements nor bias in news coverage sways individuals into accepting the views of reporters or publishers.

Nevertheless, media organizations (and in particular the journalistic profession) do enjoy various means of indirect influence over political decisions. They shape how Americans view candidates early in an election process and frame the terms of political debate. They focus the attention of regular Americans on particular social problems, influencing which issues politicians consider worthy of attention. And members of the bureaucracy often use news articles as an indirect means to communicate with each other or to learn what is going on in other parts of the government. For these reasons and others, the mass media are a critical player in the American political system.

The Evolution of the Mass Media

Mass media fall into two types: the **print media** of newspapers and magazines and the **broadcast media** of radio and television. Although most Americans got their news from newspapers and magazines in the 19th and early 20th centuries, electronic journalism, particularly TV journalism, has become dominant in the last 50 years. Today, advances in technology are blurring the distinction between the print and broadcast media. The Internet makes information available that is also published in newspapers and magazines or presented over the radio and TV.

Newspapers and magazines

The earliest newspapers in the United States were tied to political groups or parties. *The Federalist Papers,* which urged the ratification of the Constitution, were first published in New York newspapers. During George Washington's administration, the *Gazette of the United States* represented Alexander Hamilton and the Federalists, while the *National Gazette* supported Thomas Jefferson and the Democratic Republicans. The development of high-speed presses, growing literacy rates, and the invention of the telegraph led to the rise of independent, mass-circulation newspapers in the first half of the 19th century. Competition for readers and advertisers became intense, so papers increasingly emphasized the sensational side of news in the second half of that century. This style of reporting became known as **yellow journalism,** and the most well-known practitioner was William Randolph Hearst in his *New York Journal.* Its stories and reports on Cuba, particularly the explosion of the USS *Maine* in Havana Harbor, helped build support for the war against Spain in 1898. Although there was a decided shift to objective and balanced reporting in reaction to Hearst's style, this type of journalism continues in the **tabloid press,** which includes some mainstream newspapers and the "supermarket papers" such as the *National Enquirer* and the *Star.*

Weekly and monthly magazines like *McClure's* and *Collier's* published in-depth articles on national issues and gained a large, middle-class audience by the late 19th century. They became an outlet for the **muckrakers,** a group of writers whose exposés on political corruption in the cities and on the practices of the Standard Oil Company were a factor in the political reforms of the Progressive Era (1900–1920). The investigative reporting that brought the Watergate scandal to the public's attention is part of the muckraking tradition in print journalism.

Radio and television

From the 1920s through the end of World War II, radio was a popular source of news and political analysis. President Franklin Roosevelt used his radio "fireside chats" (1933–1944) to speak directly to the American people about issues facing the country. Both before and during the war, radio—particularly Edward R. Murrow's broadcasts from London—was an important source of information on developments in Europe and the

Pacific. The medium has gone through a resurgence in recent years with both commercial and public (National Public Radio) all-news stations, radio talk shows, and the president's weekly radio address to the nation.

In addition to giving people news and information programming, television has allowed Americans insight into the political process and has actually become part of the process. The Democratic and Republican National Conventions were televised for the first time in 1952. Dwight Eisenhower ran the first political TV ads during his campaign. It is generally believed that John Kennedy "won" the 1960 presidential debate because he looked better than Richard Nixon on television. By bringing the Vietnam War into our homes every evening, television certainly influenced the attitudes of Americans toward the conflict and increased support for withdrawal. The advent of cable and satellite TV has also provided a means for Americans to see how their government operates. In many communities, local educational stations broadcast school board and city council proceedings. Congressional hearings and debates are available on C-SPAN, while CourtTV covers major trials.

The Structure of the Mass Media and Government Regulation

For the most part, the mass media in the United States are privately owned. Public radio and public television, which receive part of their revenues from the federal government through the Corporation for Public Broadcasting (CPB), represent a comparatively small share of the market. Private ownership ensures considerable, but not absolute, freedom from government oversight. It does raise questions, however, about how the mass media operate.

Concentration in the mass media

As a result of competition, increasing costs, and mergers, the number of newspapers in the United States has dropped sharply. Many major cities are served by only one daily paper. In addition, the number of independent newspapers has declined as chains such as Gannett purchase additional properties. At issue is whether concentration discourages diversity of opinion and ultimately leads to the management of the news by media corporations. This question seems less of a concern in the broadcast media. While there are three major TV networks (ABC, CBS, and NBC), they do not own their own affiliate stations, and they face real competition from new networks, such as Fox Television and the Cable News Network (CNN). For television, private ownership has a different impact on the nature of news programming.

Hard news vs. entertainment

Television is audience driven. The larger the audience, the higher the rates charged for commercial time and the greater the profits. Critics have charged that this situation reduces hard news coverage and requires flashier packaging of the news. For example, local TV stations give considerably less airtime to political news than to the weather report, sport scores, and human interest stories. Programs such as *Hard Copy* and *Inside Edition* are often criticized for being "tabloid" TV journalism, in which the entertainment value is more important than the news value.

Newspapers and magazines are largely protected from government interference by the First Amendment. In 1971, the Nixon administration attempted to prevent *The New York Times* and *The Washington Post* from publishing the **Pentagon Papers,** classified documents on American policy in Vietnam. The Supreme Court refused to block their publication, noting that **prior restraint** was a violation of freedom of the press. The press cannot print stories that are known to be false or are intentionally damaging to a person's reputation, however. Content is also controlled by obscenity statutes.

Regulation of radio and television

Practically from its inception, the broadcast media has been subject to regulation. During the early days of radio, stations operated on the same frequencies and often jammed each other's signals. The Federal Radio Act (1927) set up licensing procedures to allocate frequencies under the premise that the airwaves belong to the public. The current regulatory framework was established by the 1934 Federal Communications Act, which established the **Federal Communications Commission (FCC).**

The FCC regulates the industry in several ways. It limits the number of radio and television stations a company can own, has rules governing public service and local programming, and reviews station operations as part of licensing process. Under the **equal time rule,** stations are required to give all candidates for political office access to airtime on the same terms. The **fairness doctrine** obligated broadcasters to present conflicting points of view on important public issues, but the FCC abolished the doctrine in 1987 with the support of President Ronald Reagan for two reasons: 1) it was considered a violation of freedom of the press, and 2) competition in the broadcast media ensured diversity of opinion.

The Functions of the Mass Media

Almost everyone gets his or her information about world, national, and local affairs from the mass media. This fact gives both print and broadcast journalism important functions that include influencing public opinion, determining the political agenda, providing a link between the government and the people, acting as a government watchdog, and affecting socialization.

Public opinion

The mass media not only report the results of public opinion surveys conducted by outside organizations but also increasingly incorporate their own polls into their news coverage. More important, newspapers and television help shape public opinion as well. Research has shown that the positions Americans take on critical issues are influenced by the media, especially when the media air divergent views and provide in-depth analysis.

Political agenda

The term *political agenda* is broader in scope than the term "public opinion," and it refers to the issues Americans think are the most important and that government needs to address. A person's perception of such matters as crime, civil rights, the economy, immigration, and welfare are affected by the manner and extent of media coverage. Studies indicate that a correlation exists between the significance people assign a problem and the frequency and amount of space or time newspapers, magazines, and television give to it.

Link between the government and the people

The mass media is the vehicle through which the government informs, explains, and tries to win support for its programs and policies. President Roosevelt's "fireside chats" used radio in this manner. Today, the major networks do not always give the president desired airtime if they believe the purpose is essentially political. If they do grant the time, the opposition party usually has the opportunity to rebut what the president says or present its own views on a topic immediately after the president speaks.

Government watchdog

From muckraking early in the century to today's investigative reporting, an important function of the mass media is to bring to the attention of the American people evidence of corruption, abuse of power, and ineffective policies and programs. Watergate would have remained just another burglary buried in the back pages of *The Washington Post* had Carl Bernstein and Bob Woodward not dug into the story. Although the media are often accused of having a "liberal bias," and indeed surveys show most journalists to be liberal Democrats, all presidential administrations face close scrutiny from print and broadcast journalists.

Socialization

The mass media, most significantly through its news, reporting, and analysis, affects what and how we learn about politics and our own political views. Along with family, schools, and religious organizations, television also becomes part of the process by which people learn society's values and come to understand what society expects from them. In this regard, the impact comes primarily from entertainment programming. Television's portrayal of minorities and women, family relations, and the place of religion in American life is considered to be a powerful influence on our attitudes.

Some people believe that Americans, especially children, imitate behavior observed in media communications. They are therefore concerned about the quantity of sex and violence on TV. This theory of behavior may be naive, and certainly it lacks consistent or weighty scientific evidence. Nevertheless, the perspective is a significant political force, because it links social conservatives who disapprove of sexual promiscuity with social liberals who find America's gun culture distasteful. Both the legislative and executive branches have pressured networks to clean up what former Vice President Al Gore called the "cultural wasteland."

The Mass Media and Political Coverage

Our prime source of political news is the mass media. But as noted earlier, comparatively little time is devoted to it on the local TV news. The same can be said of the space in many newspapers. Network broadcasts, which have the largest audience, are limited to a half hour and can only briefly report even major stories. More detailed coverage and analysis are available from cable news stations and programs like *Meet the Press.*

The focus of political coverage is on the president; whatever the president says or does is newsworthy. Part of the White House press corps always travels with the president to make sure every word and deed is immediately reported. With the exception of the most sensational deliberations of Congress or the courts (the confirmation hearings of Supreme Court nominee Clarence Thomas and the O.J. Simpson trials, for example), the media give less attention to the other branches of government. Cable television has more recently filled this void. The House of Representatives allowed

TV coverage in 1979, and the Senate allowed it in 1986 through C-SPAN. CourtTV gives Americans insight into the workings of the judicial system. Whether TV cameras are allowed in a courtroom is up to the judge, and there has been a reluctance to grant permission in the wake of the Simpson criminal trial.

How reporters get the news

Journalists rely heavily on the information they receive directly from elected officials, their aides, and press secretaries. These individuals are interested in giving their story the right **spin,** that is, presenting the information in a way that puts them, their boss, and his or her programs in the best possible light. Reporters covering the White House get press releases and a daily briefing from the president's press secretary. They also have the opportunity to question members of the administration and the president at news conferences. A presidential news conference is packaged. The president may spend hours rehearsing answers to questions that the staff thinks are the most likely to be asked.

Access to government officials is essential to reporters, and in return, they are expected to follow several unwritten rules. A White House staff person may agree to speak with a reporter only *on background,* which means that the source cannot be identified. This is why so many news stories quote "a senior White House official" or "sources within the administration." Information that is given *off the record* cannot be reported at all. **Leaks,** the unauthorized release of information to the press, are a fact of political life. In fact, sometimes officials intentionally leak a story in order to advance an administration's policies.

The media and presidential elections

The election of a president is a media event in which literally thousands of reporters descend on the states with early primary elections. Rather than concentrating on the issues and the candidates' programs, the reporters' coverage tends to stress which candidate is ahead or where each stands with a particular group of voters. This focus on the "horse race" has led media organizations to invest in repeated opinion polls during the campaign. Along the same line, the reporting of televised presidential debates emphasizes who "won" and "lost" and not the ideas that were exchanged.

In addition to hiring pollsters, presidential candidates employ media consultants who are responsible for presenting them and their messages in the most effective way. Media consultants understand that even in an election year, airtime on the nightly news is limited. The **sound bite,** a term that describes a politician's succinct remark, fits well into this limited format. These strategists also design the candidates' television advertising campaigns. Although the public and the media often complain about it, **negative advertising** works. A negative ad is one that focuses on what opponents have done or the positions they have taken rather than on the candidates' own views, and it often distorts the record. George Bush effectively used a photograph of Willie Horton, a rapist who committed murder while on a release program, to stress that Michael Dukakis was soft on crime.

The expansion of radio and television talk shows has given candidates access to more free airtime. An appearance by a presidential contender assures such programs instant ratings, and it gives candidates an opportunity to speak directly to the American people without having their statements analyzed by broadcast journalists. A similar advantage is gained from the so-called **infomercial,** in which candidates buy a half-hour block of time to explain their positions, although the costs are significant. H. Ross Perot used both of these longer formats quite successfully in the 1992 campaign.

Chapter Checkout

Q&A

1. When a source gives reporters information that they can use in news reports, as long as they do not identify exactly who provided it, the information is said to be given

   a. on background.
   b. off the record.
   c. through a leak.
   d. on infomercial.
   e. by strange bedfellows.

2. True or False: The First Amendment gives almost complete freedom of the press to print media, but broadcasters still face government regulation because they use the public airwaves.

3. The muckraker tradition of hard-hitting investigative journalism in weekly and monthly news magazines helped produced the reform movements of the _____ Era.

4. The sensational approach to news reporting that dominated publications owned by William Randolph Hearst, often called _____ journalism, still appears in many tabloid periodicals available in supermarket lines and urban newsstands.

Answers: 1. a **2.** T **3.** Progressive **4.** yellow

Chapter 9

POLITICAL PARTIES

Chapter Check-In

❑ Tracing the history of political parties

❑ Understanding the structure and functions of parties

❑ Considering why two parties can dominate government

Political parties perform an important task in government. They bring people together to achieve control of the government, develop policies favorable to their interests or the groups that support them, and organize and persuade voters to elect their candidates to office. Although very much involved in the operation of government at all levels, political parties are not the government itself, and the Constitution makes no mention of them.

The Functions of Political Parties

The basic purpose of political parties is to nominate candidates for public office and to get as many of them elected as possible. Once elected, these officials try to achieve the goals of their party through legislation and program initiatives. Although many people do not think of it this way, registering as a Democrat or Republican makes them members of a political party. Political parties want as many people involved as possible. Most members take a fairly passive role, simply voting for their party's candidates at election time. Some become more active and work as officials in the party or volunteer to persuade people to vote. The most ambitious members may decide to run for office themselves.

Representing groups of interests

The people represented by elected officials are called **constituents.** Whether Republican or Democrat, constituents make their concerns known to their representatives. In turn, elected officials must not only reflect the concerns of their own political party but must also try to attract support from people in their districts or states who belong to the other party. They can attract this support by supporting **bipartisan** issues, matters of concern that cross party lines, and **nonpartisan** issues, matters that have nothing to do with party allegiance.

Political parties represent groups as well as individuals. These interest groups have special concerns. They may represent the interests of farm workers, urban African Americans, small business operators, particular industries, or teachers—any similar individuals who cooperate to express a specific agenda.

Simplifying choices

The two main political parties in the United States appeal to as many different groups as possible. They do so by stating their goals in a general way so that voters are attracted to a broad philosophy without necessarily focusing on every specific issue. Republicans are known for their support of business, conservative positions on social issues, and concern about the size of government; Democrats traditionally have supported labor and minorities and believe that government can solve many of the nation's problems. The alternative to using the general philosophies of the political parties to sort out candidates is to vote for individuals based on just their own one-or two-issue programs.

Making policy

Political parties are not policymaking organizations in themselves. They certainly take positions on important policy questions, especially to provide alternatives to the position of whichever party is in power. When in power, a party attempts to put its philosophy into practice through legislation. If a candidate wins office by a large majority, it may mean that the voters have given him or her a **mandate** to carry out the program outlined in the campaign. Because President Bill Clinton failed to win a majority of the popular vote in both 1992 and 1996, few considered his victories a mandate for any specific policy or ideology. President George W. Bush also entered office without a clear mandate, because his opponent, Al Gore, won more votes (and might have won the Electoral College if not for irregularities, such as confusing ballots, in Florida).

The Development of Political Parties

The United States has a two-party system. The existence of only two dominant parties stems largely from election rules that provide for **single-member districts** and **winner-take-all elections.** Each "district" can have only one winner in any election, the person who receives the most votes. So no matter how popular a third party, it will not win a single seat in any legislature until it becomes powerful enough in a single district to take an election. By contrast, many democracies have **proportional representation,** in which officials are elected based on the percentage of votes their parties receive, and more than two dominant parties. If a party wins 10 percent of the vote in an election where 100 seats are at stake, it gets to have 10 of the seats. In a multiparty system, parties may form a *coalition,* an alliance between parties, to pool their votes if there is agreement on a major issue. Proportional representation encourages the formation of parties that are based on narrowly defined interests.

The Electoral College is also a factor in sustaining the two-party system. Even if the popular vote in a state is very close, the winner gets all of the state's electoral votes. This arrangement makes it extremely difficult for a third party to win. In the 1992 presidential election, Ross Perot captured almost 20 percent of the popular vote across the country but did not receive a single electoral vote.

The Federalists and the Democratic Republicans

Although the Constitution does not provide for political parties, two factions quickly emerged. One group, led by John Adams and Alexander Hamilton, favored business development, a strong national government, and a loose interpretation of the Constitution. The followers of Thomas Jefferson, known as Democratic Republicans, called for a society based on small farms, a relatively weak central government, and a strict interpretation of the Constitution.

The election of 1800 had constitutional implications. The Democratic Republicans chose Jefferson for president and Aaron Burr for vice president. The party's electors split their ballots for both men, resulting in a tie that was resolved in the House of Representatives. The Twelfth Amendment (1804), which required electors to vote separately for president and vice president, recognized that political parties would nominate one candidate for each office.

Jacksonian Democrats and the Whigs

During the 1820s, with the country expanding and many states dropping their property qualifications for voting, the size of the electorate grew. Andrew Jackson took advantage of this change, and from his election in 1828, the Democrats represented an alliance of small farmers, Westerners, and "mechanics," the term used for the working class. The **Whig Party**

(1834) supported business, a national bank, and a strong central government. When the Whigs broke up in the 1850s, they were replaced by the Republican Party.

This period saw important changes in how political parties operate. In the presidential election of 1832, candidates were chosen through a national convention of representatives from the states' parties, and a **party platform,** a statement of the party's beliefs and goals, was issued.

Democrats and Republicans

The Civil War split the political parties in several ways. The Republican party's strength lay in the North; Abraham Lincoln did not receive a single electoral vote from a Southern state in 1860. The Democrats in the North divided into *War Democrats,* who supported the war effort but claimed the Republicans were doing a poor job of leading the Union, and the *Peace Democrats,* or **Copperheads,** who opposed the war and were suspected of disloyalty to the Union. To win the election of 1864, the Republicans reorganized themselves as the **Union party** to attract votes from the War Democrats and nominated War Democrat Andrew Johnson for vice president. When Lincoln was assassinated, Democrat Johnson became president.

Following the Civil War, Republicans moved quickly to consolidate their control of the United States government. They quickly added a series of Western states to the Union, states that they expected would remain firm in their support for Republicans. They also set up (often corrupt) governments in the South that would regulate state elections in a manner beneficial to the party. Their record was mixed. The Democrats and Republicans alternated control of Congress, but only two Democratic presidents—Grover Cleveland (1884–1888, 1892–1896) and Woodrow Wilson (1912–1920)—were elected up to 1932. The Republican party's pro-business positions played well in the industrial North and Midwest, while the Democrats held the "solid South." The large number of immigrants who came to the United States, together with the growing industrial work force, laid the basis for strong, largely Democratic political machines in New York, Chicago, and other large cities.

The New Deal coalition and Republican resurgence

The Great Depression brought about a major shift in political party allegiance. African-American voters, who had traditionally supported the Republicans since Reconstruction, now joined the unemployed, the immigrants and their descendants, the liberal intellectuals, and the South in backing Franklin Roosevelt. The Democratic party's New Deal coalition redefined the role of the federal government as an active agent in promoting the general welfare. The Democrats dominated national politics for the next 20 years. Roosevelt's New Deal was followed by Harry Truman's Fair Deal; Republican Dwight Eisenhower (1952–1960) found it impossible to dismantle the New Deal agencies that had become an integral part of American society.

Democratic dominance collapsed in the 1960s. Young radicals turned away from liberalism in response to the Vietnam War, while moderate Democrats increasingly blamed their party for the rise of lawlessness that had accompanied liberal social change during the decade—especially the explosion of urban rioting that devastated American cities starting in 1964. From the 1968 election of Richard Nixon to Bill Clinton's 1992 victory, only one Democrat attained the White House: Jimmy Carter, whose term spanned 1976 to 1980. This succession of Republicans was due in part to the party's Southern strategy, which began to bring Southern states into the Republican column in presidential elections. Not until 1994 were Republicans able to consolidate their power by capturing control of Congress, the first time they had held both the House and the Senate in almost half a century. It is not clear whether this success is likely to continue, however, because groups who tend to support the Democrats are growing rapidly, especially the immigrant Hispanic population in the Southwest. The continuing strength of the *Grand Old Party* (or GOP) may depend upon President George W. Bush's success at reaching out to moderate minority voters.

Third Parties in American Politics

The electoral system in the United States works against a proliferation of political parties. This fact has not prevented minor parties or independents from running for office at the local, state, and national levels, however. In the 1992 national election, for example, 23 candidates ran for president. Third parties are created for a variety of reasons, and they have had an impact on American politics.

Splits within the Republican and Democratic parties

Third parties often represent factions that break away from the major parties over policy issues. These breakaway third parties have been the most successful in terms of gaining popular and Electoral College votes. In 1912, former Republican President Teddy Roosevelt ran for the White House for the **Bull-Moose party** against Republican incumbent William Howard

Taft. Opposed to Harry Truman's civil rights program, Strom Thurmond bolted the Democratic party in 1948 and became the candidate of the **States' Rights party.** Similar concerns led George Wallace of Alabama to run for president in 1968 under the banner of the **American Independent party.**

Farmer–labor parties

The **Populist party** (also known as the **People's party**) was formed by unhappy farmers, Western mining interests, and Southerners. It won a number of seats in Congress and won electoral votes in 1892. The Populists supported the Democratic candidate William Jennings Bryan in 1896, effectively committing political suicide. The coalition between farm and labor groups was revived by the **Progressive party** in 1924.

Ideological and one–issue parties

Ideological and one-issue parties may cover both ends of the political spectrum. In the presidential elections between 1904 and 1920, the **Socialist party's** candidates received between 400,000 and 900,000 votes. More recently, the most influential "party of ideas" is the **Libertarian party,** which links social liberals and economic conservatives into an alliance against government activism in all spheres of life. Although seldom successful at winning office, the party has been growing steadily; candidate Harry Browne appeared on the ballot in every state in the 2000 presidential election. In addition, political parties are formed around single issues—the **American party** (also known as the **Know-Nothing party**) campaigned for an end to immigration to the United States in the 1850s, and the **Prohibition party**, which ran candidates well into the 1950s, opposed the consumption of alcoholic beverages.

H. Ross Perot's 1992 campaign revealed the potential power of an independent candidate with a strong base of financial support. His success in winning about 20 percent of the popular vote in 1992 neither produced comparable support in the Electoral College nor changed the results of that year's election. However, Perot's campaign had a significant impact on American politics because it forced President Clinton to devote greater attention to the nation's budget deficit, one issue that Perot had used to great advantage. As with most third parties, Perot's movement fell apart after the major parties started co-opting its issues. Perot's "United We Stand" organization paved the way for the **Reform party,** but it was taken over in the 2000 election by right-wing supporters of Patrick Buchanan, a candidate whose only clear common ground with Perot was opposition to free trade.

Ralph Nader's **Green party** candidacy attracted many fewer votes in the 2000 election than Perot did in 1992, but ultimately may have had more impact. It is hard to say exactly how many Nader supporters would not have voted if he had not been in the race. But Nader's liberal profile certainly drew more votes from Vice President Al Gore than from Texas Governor George W. Bush, and it is quite likely that this opposition from the left cost Gore enough votes to swing the election. Nader is probably the first third-party candidate since Teddy Roosevelt in 1912 to have won enough votes to affect the outcome of a presidential election.

Why third parties fail

People typically vote for a third-party candidate because they are trying to send a message to the major parties. That protest vote is often heard. Both the Democrats and Republicans have accepted reforms and programs that originally seemed radical when presented by third parties. The eight-hour workday, women's suffrage, and the railroad rate regulation are good examples. Historically, third parties eventually fail to maintain themselves at the local and state levels, usually because one of the major parties skims off their talent by embracing some of the issues that party supporters hold dear. The Populists, Progressives, and Socialists succeeded for a time in winning local and state elections, and even some congressional seats, but their numbers were too small to have a dominating influence. Third parties lack the financial resources to mount effective campaigns. Today, the cost of running for office is staggering. The two major parties consolidate their dominance of the political system by staging high-profile primaries and national conventions subsidized by taxpayer money. They exclude third-party candidates from most debates, especially those for national office. Although he held around 5 percent support in the polls, for example, Ralph Nader could not participate in the 2000 presidential debates. Indeed, he was not even allowed to sit in the audience, despite possessing a ticket!

The Structure of Political Parties

The major political parties are organized at the local (usually county), state, and national levels. Party leaders and activists are involved in choosing people to run for office, managing and financing campaigns, and developing positions and policies that appeal to party constituents. The national party organizations play key roles in presidential elections.

Local party organization

Political parties operate at the local level in municipal and county elections (though many cities choose officials—mayors and members of city council—through **nonpartisan elections,** in which candidates effectively run as independents without party affiliation). In *partisan elections,* the party is involved in identifying candidates, providing professional staff, and taking positions on issues of immediate concern to voters. The party leadership recognizes that the interaction between party workers, candidates, and voters is important.

In the late 19th century on through a good part of the 20th century, **political machines** flourished in several large cities; Tammany Hall in New York, Frank Hague in Jersey City, the Pendergast family in Kansas City, and Richard Daley in Chicago are examples. The political bosses, the mayors, and the party leaders used their control of patronage jobs to reward party loyalty and provide a broad range of social services. Reforms in the civil service and the growth of primary elections gradually brought an end to machine politics.

State party organization

Political parties prepare for statewide elections. Party activists are named as electors in the Electoral College if their party carries the state in a presidential election. Candidates for state office may be chosen through a primary election, state convention, or caucus process. At a state **caucus,** party members select their candidates. In many states, the executive officials—governor, lieutenant governor, treasurer, and attorney general—are elected as individuals. Although the party's **slate,** its candidates for office, is listed on the ballot, voters can vote for any candidate they want. In such states, it is not unusual for voters to elect a Democratic governor and a Republican lieutenant governor or vice versa.

National party organization

At the national level, political parties run candidates for Congress and the presidency. Each party has its own national committee made up of party leaders, elected officials, and the chairs of the state party organizations. The chair of the national committee is chosen by the party's candidate for president. The Democratic and Republican National Committees do not run the campaigns of their respective presidential candidates; they play a supporting role to the campaign organizations of the candidates themselves. In both the Senate and the House, each party has its own **congressional campaign committee,** which raises money for congressional elections.

The national convention

The national committee loosely runs the party between national conventions. As noted earlier, a party's choices for president and vice president are nominated at the national convention. The delegates to the convention are already committed to vote for particular candidates based on the results of the state primary or caucus voting. The delegates may be appointed by the state party organization, or they may have been elected through the primary process. The party works on and announces its **platform** at the national convention. The platform is made up of **planks** that explain how the party stands on the issues facing the country. The terms "platform" and "plank" date from the presidential election of 1832, when national party conventions were first held. Developing the platform is often the most controversial part of the convention. The Republicans, for example, have had to work out an acceptable compromise on abortion between pro-choice and pro-life forces within the party.

The Strengths and Weaknesses of Political Parties

Political parties have unified groups of people and helped them seek and achieve common goals. They have a tradition of participation in democratic government that is two centuries old. Political parties have not, however, stemmed the decline in the number of people who vote. Many people view the primary elections as elimination contests that have little to do with political parties. TV ads and money from political action committees (PACs) seem to do more to persuade voters than the efforts of political parties.

Political parties today better reflect American society than they did a generation ago. Men and women from all ethnic and religious groups and from all walks of life participate in party caucuses and conventions. The primary system, whatever its defects, offers far more choices to voters than did the old party machines. This openness shows that political parties have had the strength and flexibility to adapt to changing times.

Chapter Checkout

Q&A

1. True or False: Despite receiving around 20 percent of the vote in 1992, Ross Perot did not have any real effect on American politics because he could not win electoral votes.

2. Parties try to attract voter support by announcing their issue preferences as a series of planks in a comprehensive party _____.

3. When candidates win by an overwhelming margin, it is common to say that they have received a clear _____ from the voters in favor of their political platform.

Answers: 1. F (prompted focus on deficit reduction) **2.** platform **3.** mandate

Chapter 10

VOTING AND ELECTIONS

Chapter Check-In

❑ Tracking the expansion of voting rights in America

❑ Probing why Americans do not vote

❑ Exploring how voters choose who will get their vote

❑ Understanding the American election process

In a democratic society, it is the citizens' responsibility to vote in elections; the vote of a street cleaner counts just as much as the vote of a millionaire. The right to vote is the right to determine who governs. For many years, however, large numbers of Americans were denied this basic right. Today, even with all the formal restrictions against voting eliminated, a significant percentage of Americans choose not to cast their ballots. Voter participation has generally declined since 1960.

The Expansion of Suffrage

The term **suffrage,** or **franchise,** means the right to vote. Under the Constitution, residency requirements and other qualifications for voting were set by the states. In the late 18th century, it was widely held that only the best-educated men of substance were capable of making the correct voting decisions, and therefore the right to vote was limited to white male property owners. Poor white men, women, and slaves were excluded.

Universal manhood suffrage

The first breakthrough in the crusade to end voting restrictions took place in the 1820s and 1830s, when many states revised and liberalized their constitutions. During this period, often called the "Age of the Common Man" or the "Age of Jackson," property qualifications and religious tests that denied the right to vote to Catholics and Jews were removed in some states. **Universal manhood suffrage** is a little misleading, because the franchise was denied to African Americans almost everywhere.

Expansion by amendment

The right to vote was extended through the amendment process. Under the Fifteenth Amendment (1870), a person could not be denied the right to vote because of "race, color, or previous condition of servitude." In theory, this applied to all African Americans and former slaves. The long campaign for women's suffrage, which began in the 19th century with such leaders as Susan B. Anthony and Elizabeth Cady Stanton, culminated in the Nineteenth Amendment (1920). The only state that gave 18-year-olds the right to vote was Georgia; all other states set the age at 21. During the Vietnam War, the sentiment grew that if 18-year-olds were old enough to die for their country, they were old enough to vote. The Twenty-sixth Amendment (1971) lowered the voting age to 18.

Obstacles to Voting

Despite the expansion of the franchise, obstacles to voting remained, particularly for African Americans. With the power to set registration procedures, states found it relatively easy to deny African Americans the right to vote in spite of the Fifteenth Amendment.

Poll taxes

Southern states charged a fee before a person could vote, and a few added the unpaid fees from one election to another. This practice effectively disenfranchised poor African Americans and whites. The poll tax was finally abolished in 1964 through the Twenty-fourth Amendment.

Literacy tests

Again in the Southern states, literacy tests were used to restrict applicants. The usual practice was to require an African American to explain some complex part of the Constitution, while whites were given an easier passage to read and explain.

Good-character tests

Prospective African-American voters in the South had to provide an endorsement of their "good character" from two or more registered voters.

Grandfather clause

In order to register, an applicant had to prove that is or her father or grandfather had voted. Because the fathers and grandfathers of African

Americans in the South had been slaves and obviously had not voted, such applicants were rejected.

Residency requirements

Voters would have to live in a community for a certain length of time before they could vote there. In the Southern states, this was a burden to many rural blacks because they moved from job to job as farm laborers.

Other restrictions to voting

Although all the limitations on African Americans' voting have been abolished, they were not the only group affected by restrictions. Native Americans became eligible to vote in 1924 when they were made citizens of the United States by an act of Congress. It was not until 1952 that Congress overturned 19th-century laws that had denied citizenship to Asian immigrants.

Even today, voter registration requirements make it difficult, if not impossible, for some people to vote. In order to register, an applicant must have a permanent address, which the homeless do not have. Thousands of college students who go away to school can vote only "back home" through an **absentee ballot.** Many Americans find voting a chore because they move homes rapidly, and renewing their voter registration in the new locale is not a high priority.

Voter Turnout

The number of registered voters in the United States who actually vote is very low. Only about 105 million voters cast ballots in the 2000 presidential election, despite an adult population of almost 206 million people. Presidential elections spark maximum voter interest. Voter turnout in **midterm elections,** when all the seats in the House of Representatives and a third of those in the Senate are contested, drops to as low as 35 percent, and it may be even lower in state and local elections. The United States ranks near the bottom in voter participation among the countries of the world.

The process of registering

Voting in the United States is a two-step process: A person registers to vote at one time and then casts his or her ballot at another. Registering to vote is not easy. A person may have to take time off from work, which is not an appealing idea, especially if pay is docked, and find the place to register. Although registration drives sponsored by the major political parties or groups such as the League of Women Voters help, registration is often catch-as-catch-can. Local campaigns often do not move into high gear until a month before the election. A person deciding to register at that point may find it is too late.

Voters must re-register whenever they change residences. The National Voter Registration Act of 1993, also called the Motor-Voter Law, required states to provide voter registration services when adults receive or renew their drivers' licenses. Nevertheless, people who move frequently—such as soldiers, students, and the homeless—still vote at much lower rates than other Americans.

The process of voting

Even people who take the time to register may not vote. Elections are traditionally held on a Tuesday, a workday. While the polls may be open for more than 12 hours—7 a.m. to 8 p.m., for example—many still find they do not have the time to vote. Absentee ballots are increasingly used, but the voter has to send away for one, fill it in, and mail it back, making sure that all the procedures are followed correctly. News coverage of elections also has an effect. **Exit polls** and other statistical techniques allow journalists to predict the winner of an election before the polls even close. Already knowing the winner can be a strong disincentive to vote.

Who votes and who doesn't

Political scientists have analyzed voting patterns and have found that older people with more education and higher income tend to be very active politically. Despite the passage of the Twenty-sixth Amendment, the group aged 18 to 21 years old has the lowest voting percentage. Potential voters may be satisfied with the way the government is working and see no reason to cast their ballot; something has to be seriously wrong to motivate them to go to the polls. Others are so dissatisfied with all of the candidates in a particular election that the only way they would vote is for "none of the above."

Voting Choices

When it comes to the actual elections, voters have some choice in how they cast their ballots. They may strongly support a political party and vote for that party's candidates. Voters may turn to a candidate based on his or her personality, or they may vote for or against candidates solely on their stand on a particular issue.

Voting the party line

A strong supporter of a party usually votes a straight party ticket. A Democrat votes for Democratic candidates for all elected offices, and Republicans do the same. About a quarter of the electorate votes in this way. Those with a lower sense of party identification vote more independently. They vote for a **split ticket,** choosing a Democrat for one office and a Republican for another. The major influence on party affiliation is family background. If your parents were Democrats, chances are that you will be one, too. Such commitments are often lifelong, but not rigidly so. An individual who becomes a successful businessperson may become a Republican in the belief that the party better represents his or her interests.

The personality element

Some candidates have such strong personalities that voters will cross party lines to support them. Franklin Roosevelt, Dwight Eisenhower, and Ronald Reagan exemplified high levels of personal appeal, just as Gerald Ford and Jimmy Carter did not. In looking at personality, voters may also consider such factors as character and the way candidates lead their personal life.

Issue voting

Many voters claim they vote solely on the issues, meaning that they choose a candidate by where he or she stands on questions of great importance to them. In recent years, several issues have surfaced as **litmus tests** for candidates running for office. These include such controversial subjects as abortion, immigration reform, and affirmative action. Some people simply will not vote for a candidate who takes a position on these issues contrary to their own. When two candidates share the same view on litmus-test issues, issue voters may have a difficult time deciding which person best represents their concerns.

Alternatives to voting

There are other ways to express oneself politically. Many states have adopted the **initiative** as a way of passing laws that the legislature refused or was afraid to consider. A minimum number of registered voter signatures on a petition qualifies an initiative proposal for the ballot. Originally designed as a reform measure during the Progressive Era (1900–1920) to bypass reluctant state legislatures, initiatives (also called *propositions*) have become controversial in recent years. In California, voters approved a major property tax reform through the initiative process. The California Civil Rights Initiative, passed in 1996, effectively eliminated affirmative action programs in the state. Another vehicle for voting is the **referendum,** in which a state legislature may refer a law it has approved to the electorate if the law involves the expenditure of large amounts of money or the sale of state bonds. The **recall** is provided by many states for removing incumbents from office.

In the South in the 1950s and early 1960s, most rural African Americans could not vote. They turned to political protest to express their concerns. The August 1963 march on Washington brought hundreds of thousands of people to the capital to demonstrate for civil rights. The numbers impressed President Kennedy and prompted him to take stronger action against racial bigotry. **Civil disobedience,** nonviolent action against laws that are considered unjust, was part of both the civil rights movement and the protest against the Vietnam War. People held sit-ins at restaurants that refused to serve African Americans, and young men burned their draft cards or refused induction into the armed services. Political violence has been a part of recent American history. Left-wing extremists such as the Weathermen robbed banks in the 1960s to support their protests. In the 1990s, right-wing extremists attacked abortion clinics and murdered physicians who performed abortions and blew up the federal building in Oklahoma City.

Getting Nominated and Campaigning for Office

One of the most famous images in American politics is the smoke-filled room, where the political bosses met to decide whom they would support. The bosses' power has given way to the power of the voters, who now decide on their party's nominees. Reforms during the Progressive Era started the trend toward **primary elections,** in which voters directly select their party nominees, a process that was solidified for presidential elections starting in 1972.

Primary elections

A primary is an election in which voters choose the parties' candidates for the general election. There are two types of primaries. In a **closed primary,** only a party's registered voters may vote; in an **open primary,** registered voters in either party can participate. Sometimes winning the primary is tantamount to winning the election because voter registration in the state assembly or congressional district heavily favors one party or the other.

There are often many candidates in a state or municipal primary. If one candidate does not receive a majority of the votes, the top two usually face each other in a **runoff election.**

Nominating a president

As stated in Chapter 9, each party nominates its candidate for president at the national convention. While some of the delegates are still appointed by state party leaders or are elected officials themselves, most are selected through the primary election or caucus process. Presidential primaries may be winner-take-all, in which the candidate who gets the most primary votes gets all the state's delegates, or the delegates may be divided among several candidates based on their percentage of the vote. In caucus states, delegates from the local level are selected for the county caucus, and from the county caucus they go to the state convention. Because of the primaries and caucuses, a party's nominee for president is really chosen long before the convention held in July or August. An incumbent president rarely faces a primary challenge, but Jimmy Carter did from Ted Kennedy in 1980, and so did George Bush in 1992 from Pat Buchanan.

Political campaigns

Because of the importance primaries have assumed, and because most states have been pushing their primaries earlier and earlier, the political campaign season has become longer. Candidates may announce their plans to run for president as early as two years before the election. Combined with the huge role the media play in elections, the effect of this prolonged season has been to significantly increase the cost of campaigning for office.

Until 1971, there were no controls on campaign financing. The **Federal Election Campaign Act** (1971) and subsequent amendments have limited the amount both individuals and organizations such as **political action committees (PACs)** can give to presidential candidates seeking the nomination and to the House and Senate candidates during the primary and general election campaigns. A spending limit is imposed on presidential primaries, and federal matching funds are distributed by the **Federal Election Commission** (created in 1974) to candidates who qualify by raising a certain amount of contributions on their own. The Democratic and Republican nominees for president can receive full public funding for the general election from the commission, which also oversees campaign finance disclosure requirements. The federal money comes from an income-tax checkoff that goes to the treasury's Presidential Campaign Fund. Limits on campaign spending have lost their influence over time, however, because the Supreme Court has ruled that political parties may spend unlimited **soft money**—cash that is used to build their party and that only indirectly benefits particular candidates.

Electing Candidates to Office

The culmination of the political process comes on election day when people go into the voting booths and mark their ballot for the candidate of their choice. Up to this point, most voters have been passive—they have watched the political ads on television, glanced through the campaign literature, and tried to keep up with the newspaper, radio, and TV analysis. Comparatively few have worked on a campaign or contributed money to a candidate.

As noted earlier, incumbents have many advantages when they run for reelection. Some elections have no incumbent because of resignation, death, or the creation of a new congressional or state legislative district through reapportionment. These are called **open elections.**

Electing a president

One of the most popular misconceptions regarding presidential elections is that voters directly vote for one candidate or another. What the voters actually do is choose a slate of electors in their state who make up the Electoral College. There are 538 Electoral College votes: 100 represent the two senators from each state, 435 represent the number of congressional districts, and 3 were provided to the District of Columbia by the Twenty-third Amendment (1961).

Although each state technically may decide how to choose electors, almost every state uses a winner-take-all system in which the presidential candidate with the most votes gets all of that state's electoral votes. A majority (270) of the votes in the Electoral College must be won for the candidate to be elected president. If no candidate receives a majority, the election is decided by the House of Representatives, with each state having one vote.

The Electoral College has come under particularly intense scrutiny since the 2000 election, because Vice President Al Gore won the most popular votes but narrowly lost the vote among electors. Furthermore, the closeness of the contest meant that voting irregularities in Florida, such as confusing ballots, may have cost Gore the election—and no state's election laws should decide who holds the presidency. On the other hand, some commentators say that the troublesome 2000 election showed exactly why the Electoral

College system is a good one. In such a close election, representatives of both parties would have combed through the records everywhere to find more support for their candidates. With the Electoral College, though, the parties were able to focus their battle on the legal and practical issues involved in one state's voting. Regardless of the merits on each side in this debate, ending the Electoral College would require a constitutional amendment, and therefore is unlikely to happen.

The coattails effect

A party's nominee for president is at the top of a ballot that includes candidates for the House and Senate, governor, the state legislature, and local offices. The ability of the presidential nominee to help get these other officials elected is known as the **coattails effect.** Ronald Reagan had long coattails in 1980, when enough Republicans were elected to give the party control of the Senate for the first time in a quarter century.

Congressional elections

Under the Constitution, all 435 members of the House of Representatives and a third of the senators are up for election every two years. In off-year, or *midterm,* elections, voter participation is lower than when there is a presidential contest. Although the state and local issues are important in themselves, the results may have additional national significance. Historically, midterm elections are a referendum on the performance of the administration, and the party that controls the White House almost always loses seats in Congress. Dissatisfaction with President Clinton was so great in 1994 that Republicans won control of both the House and the Senate for the first time in 40 years. But in 1998, President Clinton was the first sitting president since the 1930s whose party *gained* congressional seats in a midterm election.

Chapter Checkout

Q&A

1. Which obstacle to voting was outlawed by constitutional amendment?

    a. Poll taxes
    b. Literacy tests
    c. Residency requirements
    d. Good character tests
    e. Grandfather clauses
    f. Candidates who are not worth voting for anyway

2. When voters support all the candidates from the same party, this is often called

    a. voting a straight ticket
    b. voting a litmus test
    c. voting on personal appeal
    d. voting without standards

3. True or False: The U.S. Constitution states that the presidential candidate who wins the most votes in a state receives all of that state's electoral votes.

4. The United States has slowly expanded the _____ (or vote) to include African Americans, women, Native Americans, and adults under age 21.

Answers: 1. a **2.** a **3.** F (states choose) **4.** suffrage or franchise

Critical Thinking

1. The Electoral College usually tracks the popular vote, with the same presidential candidate winning in each. On occasion, such as in 2000, the Electoral College chooses a different candidate than the one who received the most votes. This arrangement is easy to criticize, but try to brainstorm reasons why it may be less dangerous than a straightforward election. Can you think of any other reasons why using the Electoral College is a good idea?

Chapter 11

INTEREST GROUPS

Chapter Check-In

❑ Outlining the different sorts of interest groups

❑ Considering the reasons such groups exist

❑ Examining how interest groups influence policy

Few would argue that one person could not make a difference in American politics. But there is power in numbers, and political institutions are more likely to respond to a collective rather than to an individual voice. An *interest group* is an organization whose members share common concerns and try to influence government policies affecting those concerns. Interest groups are also known as *lobbies;* lobbying is one of the ways interest groups shape legislation and bring the views of their constituents to the attention of decision-makers.

Elected officials as well as the public are often critical of the roles of "special interests" in the political process. The activities of lobbyists can smack of vote-buying and influence-peddling. There are so many organized lobbies today, representing numerous segments of society and addressing such a wide range of issue, that the distinction between "special interests" and those of the American people may no longer be valid. In a sense, interest groups are us.

Types of Interest Groups

There are 23,000 entries in the *Encyclopedia of Associations,* and a high percentage of them qualify as interest groups. Many have their national headquarters in Washington, D.C., for ready access to legislators and policymakers. Interest groups can be grouped into several broad categories.

Economic interest groups

Certainly the largest category, economic interest groups include organizations that represent big business, such as the U.S. Chamber of Commerce and the National Association of Manufacturers (NAM), as well as big labor—the American Federation of Labor and Congress of Industrial Organization (AFL-CIO) and the International Brotherhood of Teamsters, for example. Large corporations and individual unions also have offices in the capital. **Trade associations** represent entire industries. The members of the American Public Power Association (APPA), for example, are municipally owned electric utilities, rural electric cooperatives, and state power authorities. Professionals also form interest groups. The American Medical Association (AMA) opposed legislation to create health maintenance organizations for years.

Public interest groups

Public interest groups do not usually expect to profit directly from the policy changes they seek. However, the activists who staff these groups gain financially by attracting donations from individuals and foundations who support their activities. As the name implies, public interest groups enjoy an image of non-partisanship, even though some of them engage in clearly political activities (such as when Common Cause joined the fight against President George W. Bush's attorney general nominee, John Ashcroft). These groups also usually receive disproportionately positive news coverage, even when there is serious disagreement over their policy proposals. A large number of consumer advocacy groups and environmental organizations, such as the Environmental Defense Fund (EDF), fall into this category. Perhaps best known is the League of Women Voters, which promotes simplified voting procedures and an informed electorate, and Common Cause, which backs more effective government. Common Cause is a strong critic of other interest groups for their excessive campaign contributions, and it lobbies for campaign finance reform.

Government interest groups

Given the structure of our federal system, it is not surprising that there are organizations to bring the issues of local and state government before Congress and the administration. Government interest groups include the National League of Cities, the National Conference of Mayors, and the National Governors Association. One critical task performed by these groups is to help state and local governments get federal grants. These funds are important because they are a central means in which states get back money taken away through federal taxes. As the budget has tightened and as more Republicans have won governorships, these groups have become more likely to seek more local control over policies instead of more cash.

Religious interest groups

The separation of church and state does not preclude religious interest groups from lobbying. The Christian Coalition, which draws most of its support from conservative Protestants, has an agenda that includes support for school prayer, opposition to homosexual rights, and a constitutional amendment banning abortion. It became an important factor in American politics, particularly in the Republican party, in the early 1990s.

Civil rights interest groups

The National Association for the Advancement of Colored People (NAACP), the Mexican-American Legal Defense and Education Fund (MALDEF), and the National Organization for Women (NOW) represent groups that historically have faced legal discrimination and, in many respects, continue to lack equal opportunity. Their concerns involve more than civil rights, however, and encompass social welfare, immigration policy, affirmative action, and a variety of gender issues.

Ideological interest groups

Ideological interest groups view all issues—federal spending, taxes, foreign affairs, court appointments, and so forth—through the lens of their political ideology, typically liberal or conservative. Their support for legislation or policy depends exclusively on whether they find it ideologically sound. Americans for Democratic Action (ADA), a liberal group, and the American Conservative Union (ACU) rate elected officials by the same standard. A Republican challenger might point to an incumbent's high ADA rating to show that he or she is too liberal to represent the district.

Single-issue interest groups

Some interest groups are formed to advocate for or against a single issue. Although other interest groups may have a position for or against gun control, it is the only issue in the political arena for the National Rifle Association (NRA) and the National Coalition to Ban Handguns (NCBH). The same is true of abortion, which pits the National Right to Life Committee (NRLC) against the National Abortion Rights Action League (NARAL). These examples are not meant to suggest that single-issue interest groups always generate their opposite. Mothers Against Drunk Driving (MADD), which campaigns for stiffer sentences for driving while intoxicated and mandatory penalties for the first offense, clearly does not.

Functions of Interest Groups

The two principle functions of interest groups are representation and education. For example, the National Telephone Cooperative Association (NTCA), which serves telecommunications cooperatives and companies in small towns and rural areas, provides its members "aggressive representation on Capitol Hill." It also conducts educational seminars, publishes a newsletter that tracks legislative and regulatory trends, and shares expertise on marketing strategies and new technology.

Representation

The representation function stems from the reason interest groups are created in the first place: Collective action is the most effective way of influencing policymaking and bringing issues to a large audience. The specific tactics that interest groups use in representing their members, particularly before the government, are discussed later in this chapter. Interest groups also serve as a watchdog, monitoring the actions of Congress, the courts, and the administration in the interest of their constituents. This work can include keeping track of the voting record of members of Congress and rating them on how well or how poorly they do on a particular issue.

Membership itself is important to success. More than 2.5 million people belong to the NRA, and 550,000 belong to the Sierra Club. Such numbers give the organizations immediate political clout as well as the resources to maintain a large staff, hire lobbyists, and conduct extensive public relations efforts.

Interest groups are concerned with maintaining and expanding their membership. Beyond political victories, they offer special member services that may include group health and life insurance, discounts on travel, and other similar programs. **Direct mail,** which is targeted to people likely to support the interest group based on level of income and education and their other affiliations, is a way of soliciting funds and building membership rolls. Such direct mail campaigns can also put an issue before the public and help shape the political agenda of the country. All organizations appreciate, however, that some people benefit directly from what the organization does but will never become active participants or contribute money. This is known as the **free-rider problem.**

Education

Interest groups educate both their own constituency and the public. Through their publications, the groups keep members abreast of the latest developments on the issues about which they care. Business interest groups, particularly trade association, publish data and reports on their sector of the economy that are widely used. The American Petroleum Institute's tri-annual *Basic Petroleum Data Book* is an indispensable source on oil prices and production around the world. The League of Women Voters makes information available on ballot measures and the positions candidates take, and it organizes debates and issue forums. Because they have developed an expertise in a particular policy area, interest groups are often called on to testify before Congress irrespective of the position they might have on the legislation. Education is sometimes formal, as with the American Bar Association's Continuing Legal Education program, which provides attorneys with ongoing training.

Tactics of Interest Groups

Interest groups not only report developments or trends but also try to influence them in a manner that benefits their members or the cause they support. This persuasion is accomplished through lobbying, grassroots campaigns, political action committees, and litigation.

Lobbying

Lobbying efforts are directed primarily at the national level: committees of Congress that consider legislation, administrative agencies that are responsible for writing or enforcing regulations, and executive departments. Lobbyists depend on their personal relationships with members of Congress and the executive branch, which are based on keeping in regular contact. Many lobbyists have served in government themselves. This means they have worked, in some cases for years, with the very people they are now lobbying, and this experience gives them invaluable insights into how things are accomplished in Washington.

The critical legislative work in Congress takes place in committees. Lobbyists testify at committee hearings, provide the staff with information, and, more frequently than most people realize, actually write the legislation. They are sophisticated professionals and do not simply say to senators, "Vote for this bill or else," but instead explain why the bill is important to their constituency as well as what impact it will have in the senator's state. A lobbyist may have a politically connected member of the interest group contact the senator.

Important public policy decisions are made by regulatory agencies such as the Federal Communications Commission (FCC). Lobbyists or interest-group lawyers, particularly those representing corporations and trade associations, use the same tactics with agencies as they do with Congress.

Developing regulations is a multistep process that involves initial drafting, hearings and submission of comments, and the issuance of final rules. Interest groups are involved in all stages: They testify before administrative hearings, submit comments or file briefs, and draft the regulations their clients are required to operate under.

One of the criticisms of lobbyists is that they have too direct a role, based on their relationships with government officials, in how laws are written and implemented. The term **iron triangle** (also known as a **cozy triangle**) describes the ties between congressional committees, administrative agencies whose funding is set by the committees, and the lobbyists who work closely with both. Few policy areas are still governed by tightly knit subgovernments, however. Policy in areas such as telecommunications and banking generally emerges from much more complex **issue networks** involving diverse players who are united, if anything, by their expertise in the area.

Grassroots campaigns

An interest group can influence policy by marshalling its constituents and appealing to the public for support. It may urge its members to write to their representative and senator or even call them on the eve of an important vote. The NRA is known for its effective use of this tactic. Direct mail can also reach people who are not members and solicit both their backing for a particular policy and a contribution. During the debate over the North American Free Trade Agreement (NAFTA), business and organized labor mounted major print and media advertising campaigns to rally public opinion.

Groups with agendas as different as MADD's, the NRLC's, and the AFL-CIO's have organized demonstrations and protests that usually get media attention to publicize their cause. Interest groups may also directly help candidates who support their positions by providing them with campaign workers and using their own members to get people to vote; they may publicly endorse candidates for office as well as give money to the candidates' campaign funds.

Political action committees

Political action committees (PACs) are groups that raise and distribute money to candidates. They may be affiliated with an existing interest group, such as a labor union or trade association, but they can be independent. When changes in campaign financing laws in 1971 limited the amount of money an individual could contribute, PACs became a major force in American politics. The number of PACs has grown dramatically in the last 20 years, as has the amount of money they donate. Under current law, there is a $5,000 limit on PAC contributions to candidates for Congress.

PACs are not always separate from other interest groups. Often they are the campaign-financing wing of a larger lobbying effort. Among the top ten PACs, judged by their donations to campaigns in 1997–1998, are the NRA Victory Fund and PACs for the Association of Trial Lawyers, the National Education Association, and the American Medical Association. It is unclear how much the contributions actually change policy. Because most of the money goes to incumbents and because research has not turned up much evidence that members of Congress change their votes in response to contributions, many scholars doubt that the money has any direct impact. On the other hand, a member of Congress keeps a busy schedule and has little time to consider the desires of everyone. Contributions are a good way to buy time, either opening channels of access to representatives or convincing them to work hard promoting legislation.

Litigation

When Congress and the executive branch are unresponsive, interest groups can turn to the courts for remedy. The NAACP, for example, played a major role in the landmark civil rights cases of the 1950s and 1960s. Pro-life groups have filed suit in state and federal courts to limit abortions. Planned Parenthood, on the other hand, has sought injunctions against demonstrators blocking access to clinics where abortions are performed. Interest groups may be a plaintiff in a lawsuit, provide the attorneys or underwrite the costs of the legal team, or submit an *amicus curiae* brief in support of one side or another.

Regulation of Interest Groups

Interest groups have both their opponents and supporters. The critics maintain that they only give those who have considerable wealth and power additional political influence and that the tactics used and the money available corrupts the political process. The defenders argue, on the other hand, that the system is much more open than in the past and point to the effective lobbying that groups representing women, minorities, and older adults are able to do. They claim that instances of corruption are the rare exceptions, and they champion interest groups as a vehicle for Americans to petition the government. As in other areas, however, this First Amendment guarantee is not absolute. The courts have ruled that limitations on lobbying are legitimate because its goal is to directly influence legislation.

Controls over lobbying

Lobbyists are required to register with the clerk of the House and the secretary of the Senate and indicate what group they are representing, the amount of their salary or compensation, and what types of expenses are reimbursed to them. They also have to file quarterly financial statements. These controls, which admittedly have not been effective in limiting abuse, date from the 1946 Federal Regulation of Lobbying Act. In addition, lobbyists who represent foreign governments or corporations must register with the Justice Department as agents of those countries.

Congress has also attempted to slow down the so-called "revolving door" by which an official begins to lobby his or her colleagues immediately after leaving a government position. Under the 1978 Ethics in Government Act, senior executive branch officials cannot lobby federal agencies on a matter that fell within their scope of responsibility for two years after leaving government service. In addition, they are prohibited from lobbying anyone in their former agency 1) on any issue for one year and 2) forever on matters that they had been involved in.

As noted, the success of lobbyists depends on their personal ties with those in government. Those relationships are often cemented with gifts that can range from tickets to a football game to weekends at resort hotels. Congress has disclosure requirements in place, has restricted the maximum value of gifts, and is moving toward eliminating gift-giving altogether.

Controlling political action committees

Many Americans are concerned with the amount of money PACs raise and give to candidates. The public interest group Common Cause believes PACs should be abolished altogether. Short of this step, there are proposals to reduce the amount of money an individual PAC can contribute to a candidate or the total amount the candidate can accept from all PACs. Expanding federal financing of elections to include congressional races or making some provision for the government to underwrite certain types of campaign expenses would also limit the importance of PACs. For obvious reasons, Congress has not been very willing to tackle this problem.

Chapter Checkout

Q&A

1. The largest set of interest groups operating in the American political system are the

    a. economic interest groups
    b. public interest groups
    c. government interest groups
    d. ideological interest groups
    e. single-issue interest groups
    f. compounded interest groups

2. True or False: Public interest groups like Common Cause are considered apolitical because they stay out of partisan battles and do not support controversial policies.

3. A member of Congress who leaves office and immediately starts lobbying former colleagues is one example of the _____ _____ between government service and the private sector that some critics want to slow down.

Answers: 1. a **2.** F **3.** revolving door

Critical Thinking

1. Commentators often decry the role of moneyed interest groups in American politics. Underlying their criticism is a belief that everyone should have nearly equal power in political life, which a system of influence based on money does not permit. But we know from the study of voting and elections that, in fact, everyone does not enjoy equal influence. Some people find it relatively easy to stay informed, vote, or otherwise participate in politics; others find it much harder. So does the inequality created by well-funded interest groups really make the American political system worse? Can you think of a positive function that PACs might serve? Is there any justification for a system of political influence based upon wealth?

Chapter 12

CIVIL LIBERTIES

Chapter Check-In

❑ Understanding the different approaches to civil liberties

❑ Probing the guarantees included in the First Amendment

❑ Considering the rights of criminal defendants

❑ Seeking unwritten rights protected by the Constitution

Many people confuse the terms "civil liberties" and "civil rights" and use them interchangeably, even though their definitions differ. **Civil liberties** are individual freedoms and rights guaranteed to every citizen by the Bill of Rights and the due process clause of the Fourteenth Amendment. These rights include freedom of religion, speech, and the press and the considerations given to defendants accused of crimes. In recent years, such rights as privacy, abortion, and even death itself have come under the heading of civil liberties. **Civil rights,** on the other hand, deal with the protection of citizens against discrimination due to race, ethnicity, gender, or disability. These protections come from the constitutional amendments following the Bill of Rights.

An easy way to distinguish civil liberties from civil rights is to understand civil liberties as the protection of the individual from government interference. Conversely, civil rights are what people expect the government to provide to every individual, including such rights as the vote, equality in job opportunities, and equal access to housing and education. The distinction between actual civil liberties and civil rights, however, is not always so clear-cut, and many issues involve both.

Perspective on Civil Liberties

Our present understanding of civil liberties developed over time. The extent of the protection offered by the Bill of Rights and the Fourteenth Amendment has depended largely on the interpretations of the Supreme Court.

The Bill of Rights

For a century, the Bill of Rights was interpreted narrowly as protection against the abuses of the federal government. The Founders of the Constitution had the American Revolution fresh in their minds when the Bill of Rights was issued, which is why the Third Amendment, prohibiting the quartering of soldiers in homes, a non-issue today, was of great importance to them.

In the early years of the republic, the Sedition Act (1798) made it a crime to publish or say anything "false, scandalous, and malicious" against the government or its officials. The Federalists used the law to jail Republican opponents of the administration of John Adams. Today, such laws would be clearly unconstitutional, but at the time the Supreme Court was filled with unsympathetic Federalists.

Moreover, the Bill of Rights did nothing to protect citizens from abuses at the state level. While the constitutions of most states had their own Bill of Rights, enforcement of the protections varied widely.

The impact of the Fourteenth Amendment

The Fourteenth Amendment (1868) extended civil liberty protections to individuals in the states. The Supreme Court first took a limited interpretation of the amendment. The Court said that states could not take away fundamental rights without following "due process"—which the Court read as meaning simply that the states were required to follow fair procedures before, for example, incarcerating someone. Very early on, however, nationalist judges began pushing to interpret the Fourteenth Amendment as a vehicle for applying the Bill of Rights to the states. They never did win a policy of **total incorporation,** in which the first eight constitutional amendments were applied to the states in their entirety. But in 1937, the court began a formal process of **selective incorporation** through which most of the liberties contained in the Bill of Rights were declared "fundamental freedoms" applicable through the Fourteenth Amendment.

Several Bill of Rights amendments have not been applied to the states, however. The Second Amendment on the right to bear arms remains a subject of ongoing disagreement as to its meaning. The Third Amendment is obsolete. The Seventh Amendment guarantees of trial by jury in civil cases are paralleled in state laws, as is the Eighth Amendment on excessive bail and cruel and unusual punishment. The net effect of selective incorporation nonetheless has been to greatly expand the power of the federal government in protecting the civil liberties of individuals.

The First Amendment: Freedom of Religion

The First Amendment enumerates what many Americans consider to be their basic civil liberties: freedom of religion, speech, and the press and the right to peaceful assembly and to petition the government for the redress of grievances. Exactly what constitutes freedom of religion and freedom of speech are matters that have come before the courts many times.

The framers of the Constitution saw religion as a matter of choice. Unlike many countries, the United States does not have an official or state religion. Indeed, the First Amendment specifically states "Congress shall make no law respecting an establishment of religion. . . ." Nevertheless, questions on tax exemptions for religious organizations and on whether public schools should have prayer or Christmas pageants have raised thorny problems for the courts to consider.

"Wall of separation" vs. government accommodation

Thomas Jefferson believed a "wall of separation" should exist between government and religion, which meant maintaining a strict separation between church and state. Those who instead favor government accommodation argue that government can assist religion if that assistance is given in a neutral manner so that it does not favor one religious group over another nor favor religious groups in general over other groups. Both schools of thought have swayed the Supreme Court in the 20th century. Searching for a middle ground, the Court devised the **Lemon test,** based on the 1971 case *Lemon v. Kurtzman* that concerned the use of public money for a parochial school. The Court held that to be constitutional, any law has to have a secular purpose, the purpose can neither advance nor inhibit religion, and the law cannot excessively entangle government with religion. Since 1971, the Lemon test has been applied in a wide variety of cases, and although few justices endorse the doctrine unambiguously, no majority has ever come together to do more than tinker with it. As the Court has grown more conservative, its decisions have tended more toward the position of government accommodation.

Free exercise of religion

The Constitution does more than forbid "establishment" of a religion. It also guarantees that individuals will enjoy "free exercise" of their own religious beliefs. This guarantee creates a rather difficult situation, though. Policies that work too hard to accommodate the free exercise of religious beliefs stray dangerously close to establishing religion. Policies that force a sharp division between public life and private morality, on the other hand, hamper the exercise of deeply held beliefs. The Supreme Court has worked hard to formulate a constitutional doctrine that avoids either of these pitfalls, but the path is a perilous one. Current Court doctrine protects the free exercise of religion from laws that are not neutral toward a faith, such as laws banning animal sacrifice targeted at a particular religious organization. But general criminal laws, intended to promote a real governmental interest, cannot be invalidated simply because they happen to hinder the pursuit of a particular religious practice. For example, religious beliefs declaring a particular controlled substance sacred are not sufficient to exempt someone from neutral drug laws.

The list of religious issues that have come before the Supreme Court seems endless in its complexity. There are religious groups who refuse immunizations or medical help for serious illnesses and religious ceremonies in which animals are sacrificed or mind-altering drugs are used. The violations of the restrictions on prayer in the public schools are numerous. The Court has supported religious freedom and recognizes that a "wall of separation" is just too difficult to enforce.

The First Amendment: Freedom of Speech

The key question with free speech is what constitutes "speech" itself. One view separates public or political speech from private speech, holding that the latter may be limited with respect to the rights of others. The Supreme Court has protected certain kinds of speech in certain circumstances but not all kinds of speech. There are two important limitations on freedom of speech: speech cannot threaten the public order or be obscene.

Political speech

In *Schenck v. United States* (1919), Justice Oliver Wendell Holmes stated that freedom of speech could be restricted if the speech represented a **clear and present danger;** the example he gave was that a person could not shout, "Fire!" in a crowded theater that was not on fire. Through the early years of the Cold War, the clear and present danger test was used to limit the free speech of socialists and communists. The Supreme Court upheld the Smith Act (1940) that made it a crime to advocate the overthrow of the government by force. Under Chief Justice Earl Warren, the Court took the position that political speech was protected under the First Amendment unless it incited "imminent lawless action" or was "likely to produce such action."

Public speech

Nonpolitical public speech may not be to everyone's taste, and the Supreme Court has had to consider laws that restrict it. Some statements are deemed **fighting words** and are not protected. There have been cases in which a speaker was arrested because what was said might have caused a riot or a harmful disturbance. Regarding public speech, the Court has tended to approve laws that are very narrowly drawn and to reject those that paint limitations on public speech with too broad a brush.

Symbolic speech

Some forms of speech involve not words but actions, usually as part of a political protest. Examples of symbolic speech include burning the American flag and burning draft cards during the Vietnam War. The Supreme Court has sometimes protected such actions even though people might find them objectionable because they are, in effect, expressions of political ideas. In *United States v. Eichman* (1990), the Court declared the Flag Protection Act of 1989 unconstitutional on these grounds.

The First Amendment: Freedom of the Press

Freedom of the press often presents a conflict of rights. On the one hand is the public's right to know, and on the other is the right of the government to secrecy in certain circumstances, the right of individuals to privacy, and the right of defendants to a fair trial. In addition, an individual may have personal and moral sensibilities that the press should not offend. Laws tackling these polarities fall under the headings of prior restraint and subsequent punishment.

Prior restraint

Laws that call for **prior restraint** are basically censorship laws that prevent the publication of information before it is officially released. The most famous case in recent years involved the Pentagon Papers in 1971. Daniel Ellsberg, a Defense Department contractor, leaked the 47-volume report on American policy in Vietnam to *The New York Times* and *The Washington Post.* When the Nixon administration learned that the newspapers were going to publish excerpts from the report, it sought a court injunction to prevent publication. The Supreme Court ruled that prior restraint was an unconstitutional restriction on the freedom of the press.

Subsequent punishment

Subsequent punishment laws hold publications accountable for the information they publish. They may influence a publisher to think seriously about whether a story is libelous, slanderous, or obscene. Publishing statements that are malicious, untrue, and harmful to a person's reputation is called **libel.** When such statements are spoken, they are called **slander.** Celebrities and elected officials are often described negatively in the press. The Supreme Court has ruled that such stories can be considered libelous or slanderous only if it can be proved that they were published without regard for the truth or falsity of the statements. This is a difficult standard, and tabloids thrive on making outrageous claims about public figures. Recent cases have narrowed the definition of public figures, compelling the press to prove it was not malicious in making allegedly libelous statements.

Obscene materials

The Supreme Court has also maintained that obscene materials, in words or pictures, are not protected under the First Amendment. The problem is defining what is obscene. The Warren Court adopted a variable standard that set specific limits on obscenity based on the circumstances of publication and distribution. Pornography sold in an adult bookstore that limits entry to persons 21 years of age and older is legal, but showing a pornographic film to an unsuspecting audience is not. Efforts to find a clearer standard have not been successful. The Court has not been willing to turn the definition of obscenity entirely over to **community standards.** The Court has consistently found child pornography unacceptable.

The Rights of Defendants

The rights of criminal defendants are protected by the Fourth, Fifth, and Sixth Amendments to the Constitution. Although these protections are intended to shield individuals from abuses by the government, the government also has an obligation to safeguard its citizens against criminal activity. The Supreme Court has had to address both concerns.

The Fourth Amendment

The Fourth Amendment is a guarantee against unreasonable searches and seizures and requires that a search warrant be granted only with probable cause. If the police exceed their authority and conduct an illegal search, the evidence gathered may not be admissible in court under what is called the **exclusionary rule.** While initially applied only to federal cases, the rule has been extended to state courts since 1961. In recent years, the

Supreme Court has attempted to limit the exclusionary rule amid complaints that a blanket exclusion of all evidence, used even when the police error was a minor one, was letting guilty defendants go free. Under Chief Justices Warren Burger and William Rehnquist, the Court has adopted the **good faith exception** to the Fourth Amendment. This exception uses loopholes in the exclusionary rule, such as when the police believe they had a valid search warrant but it turns out to be based on outdated information. The good faith exception has been applied even to searches without warrants for which the police could show their intention was legal. Warrantless searches are based on a broad interpretation of what constitutes probable cause and a reasonable search. The overall trend has been to weaken the guarantee of personal security in favor of controlling criminal behavior.

The Fifth Amendment

The Fifth Amendment is probably one of the most misunderstood safeguards of personal liberty. In the American legal process, the burden of proof lies with the prosecution; the defendant is innocent until proven guilty and has the right to remain silent. Prosecutors can never ask the accused if he or she committed a crime. Too often, we see through news coverage of actual trials or dramatizations on film or TV someone who is obviously guilty "take the Fifth." The problem is that such a statement has, for many, come to suggest that the speaker is guilty—the exact opposite of the amendment's intent. To ensure that a person is not made a witness against himself or herself, the Supreme Court has issued several landmark rulings. *Escobedo v. Illinois* (1964) stated that a person has the right to have an attorney present when questioned by the police. In *Miranda v. Arizona* (1966), the Court required the police to inform a suspect of his or her constitutional rights. This statement by the police is now known as the **Miranda warning.**

The Sixth Amendment

The Sixth Amendment deals with the rights of the accused in criminal cases. Although a jury trial is assumed to be a fundamental civil liberty, it was not until 1968 that the Supreme Court ruled that this right is one the states are obligated to recognize in all but the most minor criminal proceedings. The states remain free to set the minimum number of people that constitute a jury, and many do not require a unanimous jury vote for conviction. In *Gideon v. Wainright* (1963), the Supreme Court held that the right to counsel provided for in the Sixth Amendment extends to the states. The government, at any level, must provide legal assistance to defendants who cannot afford their own lawyer.

Implied Rights

Some rights are not explicitly stated in the Constitution. The Ninth Amendment reads, "The enumeration in the Constitution, of certain rights, shall not be construed to deny or disparage others retained by the people." The amendment clearly leaves the door open for determining just which rights have constitutional protection.

The right to privacy

Many people believe the government has no business being involved in certain areas of people's lives. In *Griswold v. Connecticut* (1965), the Supreme Court overturned a century-old law prohibiting counseling about and on the use of birth control, noting that what goes on in a married couple's bedroom is not the concern of the state. Later decisions extended the same privacy to unmarried persons.

The privacy issue has become a subject of considerable debate. Many employers now require job applicants to be tested for drugs, as do high schools as a condition of playing on athletic teams. Considerable hysteria erupted in the mid-1980s over AIDS and whether it was a contagious disease. Lawsuits were filed over invasion of privacy when employers asked questions about their employee's sexual orientation.

The abortion issue

Until 1973, abortion was illegal in most states. In the landmark case *Roe v. Wade,* the Supreme Court stated that a woman has a right to obtain an abortion because her decision is a matter of privacy. This was not a blanket approval of abortion. In the first trimester, the decision to abort is left to the woman and her doctor. States can restrict but not ban abortions in the second trimester, and they are allowed to regulate or ban abortions altogether in the third trimester (late-term abortions) unless the procedure is necessary to save the woman's life. The case opened up numerous questions. What rights, if any, does an unborn fetus have? At what point in the pregnancy can fetal rights be assumed? Which is more important, the health of the mother or the fetus's right to life?

The Court has moved away from the *Roe* decision in recent years and has supported additional limitations on abortions unless they impose an "undue burden" on a woman attempting to exercise her privacy rights. It has upheld both state and federal statutes cutting public funds for facilities that perform abortions as well as laws that require parent notification if a minor wants an abortion. The conflict between right-to-life and pro-choice groups has sometimes led to violence, and religious and political conservatives strongly favor a constitutional amendment to ban abortions in light of the unwillingness of the Court to overturn *Roe.*

The right to die
If questions about the right of an unborn fetus to live seem complicated, the increasing age of the adult population has brought a new issue to the courts—the right to die. Modern medical technology is able to keep "alive" people who would have otherwise died. A patient may lie in a coma for years, sustained only because of life-support systems. To avoid the agony of terminal illnesses, many people write living wills, stipulating that no extraordinary measures be taken to prolong their lives.

A person who has suffered a paralyzing stroke or who is in great pain from cancer, for example, may no longer want to live. Dr. Jack Kevorkian, a Detroit physician, has helped critically ill patients end their own lives. Although some states allow assisted suicide, others call it murder. This problem demonstrates that in protecting civil liberties, the Constitution is not a static document; it responds to new and troubling questions that continue to challenge a free society.

Chapter Checkout

Q&A
1. Which constitutional amendment grants Americans a "right to privacy"?
   a. First Amendment
   b. Fourth Amendment
   c. Fifth Amendment
   d. Sixth Amendment
   e. No amendment; it's not listed in the Constitution

2. True or False: Criminal laws that make it difficult to engage in conduct sacred to your religion violate the Free Exercise clause of the First Amendment.

3. A minority of justices has wanted to apply the first eight constitutional amendments to the states through the due process clause, a position called total _____.

4. Government may impose punishments on a newspaper after it has published words lacking constitutional protection, such as libelous statements, but it may not exercise _____ _____ by preventing a publication before it gets released.

Answers: 1. e **2.** F (neutral laws are okay) **3.** incorporation **4.** prior restraint

Critical Thinking

1. The "fighting words" doctrine suggests that a speaker may be silenced because his or her words might provoke a violent reprisal from the listener. This approach to free speech effectively gives the audience the power to silence any message that they consider offensive enough to warrant violence. What do you think? To what extent should government be able to quiet someone in order to protect them from the backlash created by their own words? Is a fighting words exception to the First Amendment a dangerous loophole in protections of free expression? Or is it a reasonable relaxation of those protections, available for public authorities when they lack adequate resources to protect an unpopular minority?

Chapter 13

CIVIL RIGHTS

Chapter Check-In

❑ Connecting segregation to the institution of slavery

❑ Exploring policies intended to equalize Americans quickly

❑ Reviewing various groups that have faced discrimination

As noted in Chapter 12, civil liberties and civil rights are not the same. **Civil rights** involve the government protection of individuals against discrimination based on their race, religion, national origin, gender, age, and other factors. The concept of civil rights is based on the equal protection clause of the Fourteenth Amendment, which says that no state shall "deny to any person within its jurisdiction the equal protection of the laws."

The United States has traveled a long road in the effort to achieve equality for all its citizens. In fact, not until the middle of the 20th century did the nation take serious action to fight against discrimination. Milestones along the road show how Americans dealt with civil rights issues at various points in history.

Slavery and Civil Rights

The Declaration of Independence may have asserted that "all men are created equal," but laws clearly did not treat them that way. Slavery was a legal institution in the United States until the Thirteenth Amendment abolished it in 1865. Slavery is not specifically mentioned in the Constitution and, with the exception of the slave trade, was left to the states to deal with. The Northern states ended slavery long before the Civil War, but this did not mean that free African Americans were equal in status to whites. Laws either restricted or prevented them from voting, holding public office, serving on juries, and joining the militia.

The Missouri Compromise

By 1820, Americans recognized that the country was heading in two directions on the question of slavery. When the Missouri Territory, which allowed slavery, applied for statehood in 1819, the free states objected; the number of slave and free states was equal at that time, and the admission of Missouri would tip the balance in the Senate in favor of the proponents of slavery.

The **Missouri Compromise,** which was worked out by Henry Clay, maintained the balance by admitting Maine as a free state. Further, all territories north of latitude 36°30' north would be free. New states were admitted in pairs: Arkansas (1836) and Michigan (1837), Florida (1845) and Iowa (1846), Texas (1845) and Wisconsin (1848).

The Compromise of 1850

The territory the United States acquired at the end of the Mexican War raised the issue of the extension of slavery again. After considerable debate, Congress approved a series of laws known collectively as the **Compromise of 1850,** which admitted California as a free state, ended the slave trade in the District of Columbia, and organized the New Mexico and Utah Territories with no restrictions on slavery. The South won a fugitive slave law that made harboring an escaped slave a federal crime.

The Dred Scott decision

In the 1857 Dred Scott decision, the Supreme Court ruled that slaves must remain slaves even though they reside in a free state. Chief Justice Roger B. Taney stated that African Americans were never meant to be included in the term "citizen" in the Constitution and, therefore, had no rights under the Constitution. Further, Taney declared that the Missouri Compromise, which was the basis for Scott's claim, was unconstitutional because it denied slave owners their property rights.

The Emancipation Proclamation and the abolition of slavery

The Civil War (1861–1865) began as a test of whether states could withdraw from the Union, but the goals of the North soon broadened to include abolishing slavery. On January 1, 1863, President Abraham Lincoln, using his war powers as commander in chief, issued the Emancipation Proclamation that freed the slaves in the rebel-held areas of the country. Technically, the proclamation did not free the slaves, but it had that effect as thousands of slaves left Southern plantations. Slavery as an institution was not abolished until the end of the war with the ratification of the Thirteenth Amendment (1865), which the Southern states were required to accept as a condition for readmission to the Union.

Segregation in the United States

The end of slavery, while certainly a landmark in the history of civil rights, did not mean equality for the former slaves. At first, the Southern states used the **black codes,** local laws that limited former slaves' ability to find work and freedom to move off the plantations. In response, Congress passed the Civil Rights Act of 1866 that made African Americans citizens. This was followed by the Fourteenth and Fifteenth Amendments (1868 and 1870), which reaffirmed that African Americans are citizens, entitled to "equal protection," and have the right to vote.

African Americans soon learned that the Constitution might promise equal protection, but realizing that promise was another matter. The Supreme Court interpreted the Fourteenth Amendment very narrowly, stating that the federal government could not prosecute individuals for discriminatory acts. Lynchings and mob violence were left to the states to handle. Within a generation after the end of Reconstruction (1877), African Americans in the South found themselves deprived of their civil rights.

Jim Crow laws

Jim Crow laws were Southern statutes that effectively segregated people by race. In a group of decisions known as the Civil Rights Cases (1883), the Supreme Court struck down the Civil Rights Act of 1875 that had forbidden racial segregation in public accommodations such as hotels and trains. Under the Jim Crow laws, separate facilities for black and white train and streetcar passengers, separate schools, and separate entrances and reception areas in public buildings were built in the South. Separate restrooms and drinking fountains, as well as special visiting hours for African Americans at museums, became fixtures of Southern life. Because this separation based on race was backed by law, it was called **de jure segregation.**

Separate but equal doctrine

In 1896, Homer Plessy challenged segregation by riding in a "white only" railroad car. The case went to the Supreme Court, which ruled in *Plessy v. Ferguson* that such segregation was constitutional as long as the facilities were equal. The court's "separate but equal" doctrine was soon applied to schools as well as theaters, beaches, and sports facilities. However, separate was hardly equal. Black schools received discarded textbooks and lab equipment from white schools, and the buildings themselves were dilapidated. All facilities that were for African Americans to use were inferior.

Until the 1950s, America was a segregated society. Major-league baseball was segregated until 1947; African Americans played in the Negro Leagues. Hollywood played its part, limiting African Americans to roles as domestics or making "all-Negro" films that were shown in segregated movie theaters. The practice of segregation moved beyond the South into other parts of the country, including Chicago and Los Angeles.

African Americans were also denied the right to vote. Southern states set up poll taxes, literacy tests, the grandfather clause, and property qualifications (see Chapter 10) that reduced the number of eligible African-American voters to insignificance outside of the most urban areas.

Breaking Down Segregation

Eliminating segregation in the United States has proved to be a long and difficult process. Presidential actions and court decisions were important early steps. While segregation codified in law no longer exists, **de facto segregation** based on income and housing patterns continues.

Executive actions

The first meaningful gains in civil rights came after World War II. In 1948, President Harry Truman ordered an end to segregation in the military and the federal bureaucracy. Segregated units in the U.S. Army were disbanded within three years, and the Korean War became the first conflict in which blacks and whites truly fought side by side.

Truman ran into difficulty when he tried to push his civil rights agenda through Congress. A federal anti-lynching law, the outlawing of poll taxes, and the creation of a civil rights commission were opposed by Southern Democrats. The Courts proved to be more willing to look at these issues.

Brown v. Board of Education of Topeka

In 1950, Oliver Brown sued in federal court over the segregation of the school system of Topeka, Kansas. The Supreme Court's 1954 decision in the case, which held that separate schools were inherently unequal, was important for several reasons. Topeka was not a Southern city; the Court hoped to limit backlash in the South by using a case outside the region.

However, the Court ordered the desegregation of the schools, not their integration. Although the terms are often used synonymously, they actually have different meanings. **Desegregation** refers to eliminating laws that call for segregation; **integration** means actively designing government policies to mix different races. The *Brown* decision did not call for integration but demanded desegregation "with all deliberate speed." This language provided no specific timetable or direction in how to achieve the goal, so desegregation took decades to become a reality in many school districts. When it became clear that residential segregation would keep schools racially distinct, however, the Court began to endorse active integration policies, such as busing children to schools outside their neighborhoods, to achieve racial balance in every institution.

Issues in school desegregation

It was not until the early 1970s that the federal courts approved such remedies as busing and racial quotas. These applied, however, only to districts that had practiced legal segregation and not in instances in which segregation was the result of where different groups lived. Numerous lawsuits resulted as African Americans and other racial minorities tried to provide evidence of past discrimination. Busing, which was the main vehicle for ending segregation, was strongly attacked in both the North and the South. The imposition of busing often led to **white flight,** that is, white students leaving the public schools for private schools.

The Civil Rights Movement

Civil rights groups like the National Association for the Advancement of Colored People (NAACP), which was organized in 1909, led the fight to end discrimination by using the courts. While the *Brown* decision demonstrated their success, other tactics were needed to move the country and the government into action. Civil disobedience, boycotts, and protest demonstrations created a climate of opinion that led to legislative steps to end discrimination.

Civil disobedience

Civil disobedience means testing an unjust law by deliberately breaking it. This approach was championed by the Reverend Martin Luther King, Jr., who founded the Southern Christian Leadership Conference (SCLC). In 1955, King organized a boycott of the bus service in Montgomery, Alabama, which went on for more than a year until public transportation was desegregated. Cesar Chavez and his largely Mexican-American Farm Workers of America union led a successful national boycott against table grapes produced by nonunion growers a decade later. Sit-ins were used at white-only lunch counters in the South; African Americans who were refused service simply remained in their seats and were replaced by others when the police came to arrest them. Protest marches to publicize the inequities of discrimination were usually declared illegal by local authorities in the South and were sometimes violently dispersed. News coverage of these events dramatically increased the support for the civil rights movement and brought activists, both black and white, to the South to participate.

Civil rights legislation

The **Civil Rights Act of 1964,** which survived several challenges in the courts, prohibited employment discrimination by private businesses connected with interstate commerce, authorized the attorney general to begin school desegregation lawsuits if complaints were filed, and cut off federal funding for any program that practiced discrimination. The 1965 **Voting Rights Act** eliminated literacy tests and thus significantly increased the number of African Americans and other minorities who could vote. Discrimination on the basis of race, color, religion, national origin, or sex was banned in all forms of housing through the **Civil Rights Act of 1968.** This act has not had as great an impact as other legislation because the ability to buy or rent housing is so directly connected to income level. The civil rights laws of the 1960s have been repeatedly expanded by Congress.

Racial violence

The advance of civil rights was not accomplished without violence. The images of police in the South using fire hoses and guard dogs against protest marchers were powerful and built support for the movement. The nonviolent approach of Martin Luther King, Jr., was not accepted by all African-American leaders. The **Black Muslims** under Malcom X advocated segregation of the races and were prepared to respond to violence with violence. The **Black Panther party** called for "Black Power" and, in some communities, began stockpiling weapons. Race riots broke out in cities across the country, first a wave that spanned 1964–1965 and then a second one in 1968. Angry minority citizens, purportedly spurred on by black militants, destroyed massive amounts of property (especially in ghetto areas) and occasionally brutalized innocent bystanders.

Civil Rights for Minorities and Women

African Americans are not the only group of people who have faced overt discrimination. In the early years of the republic, Catholics and Jews were denied the right to vote in some states. The Irish, Jews, and other immigrants faced a long period of de facto discrimination in housing, educational opportunities, and employment. Nor does the civil rights struggle involve only racial minorities, as the status of the disabled, homosexuals, and women demonstrates.

Hispanic Americans

As did African Americans, Hispanic Americans found that the best way to accomplish their goals lay in organizing. The Mexican-American Legal Defense and Education Fund, the United Farm Workers union, La Raza Unida, and the League of United Latin American Citizens have campaigned for increased voter registration and greater access to education.

Native Americans

In the 1960s, Native Americans began organizing against long-standing neglect and discrimination. There was an important emphasis on overcoming stereotypes about Native Americans and recovering their heritage. The **American Indian Movement (AIM)** has been one of the most effective voices seeking to preserve Native American culture as well as raise the issues associated with land claims. Native Americans have used civil disobedience—the takeover of Alcatraz Island in 1969 and the occupation of Wounded Knee, South Dakota, in 1973—to press their claims.

Disabled Americans

The 1990 **Americans with Disabilities Act (ADA)** applied the requirements of the Civil Rights Act of 1964 to more than 40 million people. It covers those who are physically or mentally handicapped, including people with AIDS and former drug or alcohol abusers, and it guarantees protection in the areas of transportation, public accommodations, employment, and telephone services. This expansion of civil rights has recently come under fire because it often forces institutions to allocate disproportionate resources to a handful of people. The presence of a single disabled student, for example, can force a school to keep a full-time nurse on payroll or to make expensive changes in facilities and equipment. The statutory definition of "disabled" is rather loose, and people using the law for leverage sometimes do not seem to be what the sponsors had in mind when they originally wrote the legislation. Nevertheless, the disabled evoke great sympathy among the general public, so elected officials are unlikely to tamper with the rights that are now in place.

Homosexuals

Although homosexuality has "come out of the closet" in the United States, this group has not been very successful in pressing its claims against discrimination. Indeed, there is a public debate over whether what are sometimes called "lifestyle choices" warrant special status or treatment. Homosexuals are still subject to dismissal from the armed services, and Congress has refused to give legal sanction to gay marriages that would make the partners eligible for a wide range of benefits.

Women

Until the 1860s, many states restricted or prevented women from owning property. A woman's right to vote was not constitutionally protected until the ratification of the Nineteenth Amendment in 1920. It was not until the Civil Rights Act of 1964 included sex on the list of characteristics that could not be discriminated against (race, age, religion, and national origin are the others) that the door was opened for a concerted campaign against gender discrimination.

The National Organization for Women (NOW) is an important force in the women's movement. It has campaigned successfully for equal employment and pay and against sexual harassment. Although the **Equal Rights Amendment (ERA)** failed ratification, the 1972 amendments to the Civil Rights Act denied federal funding to public and private institutions that discriminated against women and required equality of sports programs for men and women in schools.

In applying the equal protection clause of the Fourteenth Amendment to women, the Supreme Court has used various standards to determine the constitutionality of laws perceived to be discriminating on the basis of sex. The **rationality test,** which maintains that a law is constitutional if a reasonable person believes there is a rational basis for it, is gradually giving way to the *heightened scrutiny test* and the **strict scrutiny test.** These put a higher burden of proof on the defendant to demonstrate that there is a "substantial" or "compelling" state interest behind the law or that it is not discriminatory.

Affirmative Action

Affirmative action remains one of the most hotly debated topics in civil rights. The term refers to a broad range of programs that are intended to correct for the past effects of discrimination through preferential recruitment and treatment, numerical goals, quotas, or set asides in employment.

In contracting with a municipal or state agency, companies that are identified as minority or women business enterprises, so-called MBE/WBE, may be given a preference over a firm owned by a white male. Affirmative action traditionally goes beyond **equality of opportunity,** long the goal of the civil rights movement, and seeks **equality of outcome.**

Reverse discrimination

In *Regents of the University of California v. Bakke* (1978), the Supreme Court ruled in a controversial 5–4 decision that setting aside a specific number of places in a medical school class for minorities violated both the Civil Rights Act of 1964 and the Fourteenth Amendment. It ordered that a white applicant initially denied admission be admitted so as to avoid **reverse discrimination.** The Court also stated that the state had an interest in promoting a diverse student body in its schools. The upshot of the Bakke decision was confusing; although obvious quotas were unconstitutional, recent Court cases have further restricted affirmative action policies, so that they may be used only to redress a past pattern of discrimination.

Challenges to affirmative action

There is little doubt that affirmative action policies have changed the face of the workplace and many of our public institutions. Perhaps contrary to expectations, the group that has been helped most by affirmative action is white women. In the 1990s, the courts struck down numerous state and federal programs that used race and gender to discriminate and have considered quotas only where there is a specific history of past discrimination. Public opinion polls show broad support for ending affirmative action. This is reflected in the 1996 ballot proposition in California known as the California Civil Rights Initiative. Although voters approved the initiative to end affirmative action programs in the state except those mandated by the federal government, the constitutionality of the measure was immediately challenged in federal court.

Chapter Checkout

Q&A

1. Martin Luther King, Jr., was the central leader of a civil rights group called the

    a. Black Muslims
    b. Student Non-Violent Coordinating Committee
    c. Southern Christian Leadership Conference
    d. Black Panthers
    e. Lutheran Synod

2. True or False: Abraham Lincoln's Emancipation Proclamation ended slavery in 1863.

3. The *Bakke* decision allowed affirmative action to promote diversity but permitted race to be only one factor among many used to make college enrollment decisions; programs could not install _____ specifying the number of African Americans who would be admitted.

4. The Black Panther Party promoted _____ _____ and sometimes armed themselves to help achieve that goal.

Answers: 1. c **2.** F (Thirteenth Amendment) **3.** quotas **4.** Black Power

Critical Thinking

1. The 1896 Supreme Court decision *Plessy v. Ferguson* allowed segregation as long as facilities for blacks and whites were "separate but equal." One justification for allowing states to keep the races separate, provided by the majority, was that government should not try to legislate morality. Given the successes of 1960s civil rights legislation, however, some now conclude that government can and should legislate morality. What do you think? Does the nation's history of redressing racial imbalances suggest more generally that government can lead citizens to better morals? Or was there something special about America's racial divide that permitted government to force a new way of thinking, a specific set of conditions that probably would not appear in other instances of government-led moral reform?

Chapter 14
PUBLIC POLICY

Chapter Check-In

❑ Following the stages of the policy process

❑ Categorizing the different sorts of policies

❑ Considering problems with regulatory and social policies

Public policy refers to the actions taken by government—its decisions that are intended to solve problems and improve the quality of life for its citizens. At the federal level, public policies are enacted to regulate industry and business, to protect citizens at home and abroad, to aid state and city governments and people such as the poor through funding programs, and to encourage social goals.

The Policymaking Process

A policy established and carried out by the government goes through several stages from inception to conclusion. These are agenda building, formulation, adoption, implementation, evaluation, and termination.

Agenda building

Before a policy can be created, a problem must exist that is called to the attention of the government. Illegal immigration, for example, has been going on for many years, but it was not until the 1990s that enough people considered it such a serious problem that it required increased government action. Another example is crime. American society tolerates a certain level of crime; however, when crime rises dramatically or is perceived to be rising dramatically, it becomes an issue for policymakers to address. Specific events can place a problem on the agenda. The flooding of a town near a river raises the question of whether homes should be allowed to be built in a floodplain. New legislation on combating terrorism was a response to the 1995 bombing of the federal building in Oklahoma City.

Formulation and adoption

Policy formulation means coming up with an approach to solving a problem. Congress, the executive branch, the courts, and interest groups may be involved. Contradictory proposals are often made. The president may have one approach to welfare reform, and the opposition-party members of Congress may have another. Policy formulation has a tangible outcome: A bill goes before Congress or a regulatory agency drafts proposed rules. The process continues with adoption. A policy is adopted when Congress passes legislation, or the regulations become final, or the Supreme Court renders a decision in a case.

Implementation

The implementation or carrying out of policy is most often accomplished by institutions other than those that formulated and adopted it. A statute usually provides just a broad outline of a policy. For example, Congress may mandate improved water quality standards, but the Environmental Protection Agency (EPA) provides the details on those standards and the procedures for measuring compliance through regulations. As noted earlier, the Supreme Court has no mechanism to enforce its decisions; other branches of government must implement its determinations. Successful implementation depends on the complexity of the policy, coordination between those putting the policy into effect, and compliance. The Supreme Court's decision in *Brown v. Board of Education* is a good example. The justices realized that desegregation was a complex issue; however, they did not provide any guidance on how to implement it "with all deliberate speed." Here, implementation depended upon the close scrutiny of circuit and appeals court judges, as well as local and state school board members who were often reluctant to push social change.

Evaluation and termination

Evaluation means determining how well a policy is working and is not an easy task. People inside and outside of government typically use **cost-benefit analysis** to try to find the answer. In other words, if the government is spending x billions of dollars on this policy, are the benefits derived from it worth the expenditure? Cost-benefit analysis is based on hard-to-come-by data that are subject to different, and sometimes contradictory, interpretations.

History has shown that once implemented, policies are difficult to terminate. When they are terminated, it is usually because the policy became obsolete, clearly did not work, or lost its support among the interest groups and elected officials that placed it on the agenda in the first place. In 1974, for example, Congress enacted a national speed limit of 55 miles per hour. It was effective in reducing highway fatalities and gasoline consumption. On the other hand, the law increased costs for the trucking industry and was widely viewed as an unwarranted federal intrusion into an area that belonged to the states to regulate. The law was repealed in 1987.

Politics and Policymaking

It is impossible to separate policymaking from politics. Many groups with different interests and their own agendas are involved in all stages of policymaking. A good example is the 1996 welfare reform legislation. Passed by the Republican-controlled Congress, the reform law contains provisions for cuts in direct federal aid and new work requirements that troubled many Democrats and organizations representing the poor. President Bill Clinton signed the bill after some hesitation and then indicated that he would seek changes in the law during the next session of Congress.

Fragmented policies

A strong case can be made that the very nature of the U.S. system of government encourages fragmented policies. The separation of powers, checks and balances, and federalism mean there is no one institution responsible for making policy. To illustrate, the federal government has a perspective on immigration reform much different from that of the governors of states mandated to provide services to a growing number of illegal immigrants. Interest groups with opposing points of view on an issue also come into the mix.

The lack of coordination among agencies responsible for implementing policy also contributes to fragmentation. For example, the Federal Bureau of Investigation (FBI), the Drug Enforcement Administration (DEA), the Customs Service, and the Coast Guard, as well as the local and state police, have responsibilities in preventing illegal drugs from entering the country. Not only do their jurisdictions overlap, but each is determined to protect its turf. Anyone who has seen how local law enforcement officers and the "feds" are portrayed on television police shows has an inkling of the problem.

Politics in Congress

The formulations and adoption of public policy can be either hampered or advanced by the way things are done in Congress. As noted in Chapter 3, bills for the construction of major public works that benefit a particular district or state, such as bridges, dams, and highways or the establishment of military bases, are known as **pork-barrel legislation.** While such programs do create jobs, they may run counter to a broader policy direction, such as the need to cut the federal budget deficit.

Often, representatives from different states and even different parties may agree to support each other's legislative agendas. A New York congressman may support a water project in Arizona in return for his Arizona colleague's vote on a mass transit appropriation for the Northeast. This practice is known as **logrolling,** and it is a way of building coalitions that may back a new policy direction.

Iron triangles and issue networks

Elected officials are not the only people involved in the politics of policy. Iron triangles were discussed in the context of the role interest groups play in Chapter 11. An **issue network** is a newer concept. It involves members of Congress, committee staff, administrative and regulatory agency directors and staff, lobbyists, executive department officials, and scholars from both the academic world and so-called "think tanks" (like the conservative American Enterprise Institute, the liberal Brookings Institution, and the libertarian Cato Institute) who work on a specific policy. An issue network is much more complex than an iron triangle, and the participants are often in conflict in spite of their common area of interest.

The role of scholars in developing a policy should not be underestimated. It is not uncommon for a congressional committee holding hearings on a welfare bill to hear testimony from economists, sociologists, and political scientists who have important insights on a problem based on years of study.

Policymaking in Action

There are three broad areas of public policy: domestic, economic, and foreign. Some political scientists would include defense policy as a fourth. In domestic affairs, there are two major categories: regulatory policy and social welfare policy. (Economic and foreign policy are discussed in Chapters 15 and 16.)

Regulatory policy

Through **regulatory policy,** the federal government supervises the actions of individuals, businesses, and government institutions. Historically, the desire for regulation grew out of widespread unhappiness with the actions of profit-making businesses. For example, railroads in the late 19th century often charged more for shipping over short distances than over long ones. This pricing made sense for their business needs, but it was politically unacceptable because the nation's numerous small farmers were more likely to send goods a short distance, and the pricing was perceived as discriminatory. This and other discriminatory rate practices led to the creation of the Interstate Commerce Commission (1887) and rate regulation. During the Progressive Era, exposés about the way the food and drug industries operated resulted in Congress's passing the Pure Food and Drug Act (1906), which created the Food and Drug Administration (FDA).

Regulatory activities include setting fair prices for goods and services; granting licenses and franchises; establishing safety standards for the workplace and transportation; providing resources, such as hydroelectric power from federal dams, and setting rates; and monitoring and enforcing compliance with statutes relating to discrimination.

The scope of regulatory policies can be seen in the array of independent commissions and agencies responsible for their implementation. The Federal Communications Commission's (FCC) role with respect to the broadcast media is noted in Chapter 8. In addition, there are the Securities and Exchange Commission (SEC), which watches over the stock markets and stock transactions; the EPA, which safeguards the environment; the Federal Energy Regulatory Commission (FERC); the Occupational Safety and Health Administration (OSHA) and Consumer Product Safety Commission (CPSC), both of which were created in response to the failure of business to adequately protect its workers and customers; and the National Transportation Safety Board (NTSB). Also, many federal regulatory agencies have their counterparts at the state, and even local, level.

Criticism of regulation and deregulation

Regulatory policy is usually criticized because of the costs it imposes on business. American consumers and workers generally bear those costs: consumers through the price of products; workers when their place of business must compete with unregulated foreign concerns. Nevertheless, setting domestic policy through regulation is tempting to federal legislators because it allows them to take action on a problem and command a change of course without directly paying for anything they order. Another concern with government regulation of industry is that policy decisions often respond to political considerations rather than technical ones, which may mean hurting businesses for no good reason, or it may give certain businesses the opportunity to manipulate regulations so that they make more profit.

Deregulation began in the 1970s and was based on the notion that regulation was suppressing economic competition. The actual record has been mixed, however. Deregulation does seem to produce greater product innovation and more new company startups, but it has also resulted in the collapse or merger of inefficient large companies. For example, the deregulation of the airline industry decreased fares as numerous small carriers went into operation. Most quickly failed, leading to greater consolidation. In the telephone industry, the deregulation that came with the breakup of AT&T has created a rash of confusing rate charges and services that many people feel are just too complicated to follow. The lack of regulation over the savings industry is seen by many as a cause of the extremely costly savings-and-loan crisis of the late 1980s. California began rationing electrical power in early 2001 in the wake of changes in the state's regulatory scheme, leading some opponents to add it to the list of deregulation's failures. However, others argue that the government never stopped interfering with state utilities, so the industry was not really deregulated.

Social welfare policy

Social welfare policy deals with the causes and effects of poverty. Just as Upton Sinclair's *The Jungle* (1906) brought the need for regulation of the meatpacking industry to the public's attention, so did Jacob Riis's *How the Other Half Lives* (1890) focus attention on urban poverty. After decades of legislation and federal programs to address the problem, Michael Harrington reminded those who read his *The Other America* in the 1960s of the persistence of poverty in our affluent society. Efforts such as Lyndon Johnson's "War on Poverty" produced only limited results. In the 1990s, more than 35 million Americans were poor, as measured by the federal definition of poverty, which is an income of less than about $14,500 per year for a nonfarm family of four.

Social Security

The first federal attempt to deal with poverty came in 1935 with the Social Security Act. Under the Social Security program, employers deduct money from the paychecks of their employers, match it with an equal amount of their own money, and then send it to the federal government to provide for a pension program. Most people think of Social Security as a form of insurance or savings—that is, they put aside the money, and it is saved for their retirement—but this impression is incorrect. Rather, Social Security uses the money paid by today's workers to cover the pensions received by today's elderly. Current workers have no tangible guarantee that society will continue redistributing wealth to the elderly when their turn comes. Indeed, as the number of able-bodied workers declines and the number of elderly increases, the Social Security program is extremely unlikely to continue paying benefits at the rate it does now.

Several changes in the Social Security program have added to its cost. Money is paid out of the pension program for disabled workers and for the survivors of deceased workers. People who were not provided for in the original legislation—the self-employed and many government workers—are now covered. Benefits are expanded to include cost-of-living adjustments known as **COLAs.** As a result of all these general benefits, payroll taxes were increased and benefits reduced in the early 1980s—yet the Social Security trust fund is still running out of money. The aging of the population has raised serious questions about the fund's long-term solvency.

The "War on Poverty"

Lyndon Johnson's "War on Poverty" focused on employment and health care for the elderly and the poor. The Economic Opportunity Act of 1964 created the Jobs Corp, the Neighborhood Youth Corps, Head Start, and community action programs that the poor had a hand in running. With the exception of Head Start, many of these projects had their funding cut as the Vietnam War escalated.

Medicare, enacted in 1965, provides basic health insurance and hospitalization coverage for people over the age of 65 and is paid for by both workers and retired persons. Under **Medicaid,** medical benefits for the poor are administered by state programs, with the federal government paying for a portion of the costs. Both programs fall far short of a comprehensive national approach to health care, yet they are already by far the biggest drain on the national treasury of anything in the federal budget.

Recent trends and challenges

Entitlements, the costs associated with such social welfare policies as Social Security and Medicare, make up more than 50 percent of the federal budget. These costs increase as more people become eligible for benefits, a situation difficult to control because it is very much tied to the aging of the population. Congress and several administrations have found it difficult to reduce or eliminate entitlements, particularly for the elderly, who are represented by a powerful lobby in the American Association of Retired Persons (AARP). Some changes have had to be made, however. In addition to increasing payroll taxes and reducing COLAs, the retirement age will be 67 by 2007.

Budget cutters have had far more success trimming aid to the poor, who lack the political clout of the elderly. The main target was a program named Aid to Families with Dependent Children (AFDC), usually just called "welfare." Critics thought that the program created a cycle of poverty by encouraging single mothers to have more babies to increase their benefits. Those babies would then grow up in poverty without adequate parental supervision and therefore either turn to crime or create more illegitimate children so that they could receive welfare. Although this myth contained only an element of truth, it made AFDC much less popular than Social Security (which enjoyed a contrary myth that the elderly were just getting back what they had paid in). President Clinton signed into a law a Republican measure replacing AFDC with a new program called Temporary Assistance for Needy Families (TANF), which was much more aggressive at forcing beneficiaries to find work.

Social welfare policy also affects other issues, such as immigration and homelessness. Federal mandates require the states to shoulder a heavy financial burden to assist immigrants. This responsibility has sparked a major debate over just what social services, if any, both legal and illegal immigrants are entitled to. The country is also trying to find a policy approach to reduce homelessness. The number of homeless in the United States has increased significantly beginning in the 1980s, due to a recession and spending cuts in public housing, drug treatment, and mental health programs.

Chapter Checkout

Q&A

1. The Food and Drug Administration (FDA) is one example of an agency engaged in shaping

   a. social welfare domestic policy
   b. regulatory domestic policy
   c. economic policy
   d. foreign and defense policy
   e. dietary policy

2. The Temporary Assistance for Needy Families program was instituted to replace a costlier social-welfare program called

   a. Social Security
   b. Medicare
   c. Medicaid
   d. AFDC
   e. Congressional salaries

3. True or False: The Social Security trust fund is where payroll taxes paid by workers are held until they retire and need the money.

4. After a program has been in place for some time, policymakers often perform a _____ analysis to determine whether it is worth the investment.

Answers: 1. b **2.** d **3.** F (pay as you go) **4.** cost-benefit

Critical Thinking

1. The government makes decisions—called "policies"—just as people do. Although you may not think of your behavior as a process, and indeed for some people the "process" is very limited, everyone has a method of making decisions. Draw a flow chart representing the six stages of policy formulation. Now draw a second flow chart beside it capturing the process that you usually follow when making personal decisions. Using yourself as an example, how does a government differ from an individual when it makes decisions? Could the government's process be improved if it approached matters more as you do? Could your process be improved if you approached matters more as the government does? Are there elements of each approach that could be synthesized into a better method than either one?

Chapter 15

ECONOMIC POLICY

Chapter Check-In

❑ Understanding the different goals of economic policy

❑ Connecting economic theories to specific policies

❑ Tracing the federal budget process

❑ Probing types of taxes and the efforts to reform them

The federal government pursues policies that strive to create a healthy economy that benefits all Americans—not an easy task. An economic policy that benefits one segment of society may be damaging to another. Keeping inflation under control by raising interest rates makes it difficult for businesses to get capital to expand and hire additional workers; the unemployment rate may go up. Low interest rates, on the other hand, can lead to inflation as spending increases; many workers find their pay raises meaningless because prices go up.

Because of the complexity of economic policy, elected officials find that the only way they can come to an agreement on any aspect of it is to work out compromises. Even a president whose party controls both houses of Congress finds it difficult to get everything the executive branch wants. Tradeoffs—for example, accepting somewhat higher inflation to keep business expansion going—are essential to economic policy.

The Goals of Economic Policy

To maintain a strong economy, the federal government seeks to accomplish three policy goals: stable prices, full employment, and economic growth. In addition to these three policy goals, the federal government has other objectives to maintain sound economic policy. These include low or stable interest rates, a balanced budget (or at least a budget with a reduced deficit from the previous budget), and a trade balance with other countries.

Stable prices

When prices for goods and services increase sharply, the value of money is reduced, and it costs more to buy the same things. This condition is called **inflation.** When inflation is kept low, prices remain at the same level. Circumstances beyond the government's control can affect prices. A prolonged drought in the corn belt or an early freeze that hits the orange crop in Florida creates shortages that lead to higher prices. Higher prices for certain critical goods, such as oil, can create inflationary prices throughout the economy.

Full employment

Absolute full employment is impossible to achieve; at any given time, people are quitting their jobs or are unable to work for a variety of reasons. An **unemployment rate,** the percentage of the labor force that is out of work, of 4 percent or less is considered full employment. The unemployment rate varies from region to region and from state to state. For example, California's rate was higher than the national average in the early 1990s because of cutbacks in the aerospace industry and companies moving out of the state.

Economic growth

Economic growth is measured by the **gross national product (GNP),** the value of goods and services produced. A thriving economy may have a GNP growth rate of 4 percent a year; a stagnant economy may grow at less than 1 percent a year. In a stagnant economy, unemployment is high, productivity is low, and jobs are hard to find. In the 1970s, the United States experienced a strange combination of high unemployment and high inflation, which is known as **stagflation.**

Theories of Economic Policy

In developing an economic policy, government officials rely on the recommendations of economists who typically base their analyses on theories of how the economy works or should work. As might be expected, economists often disagree on the cause of a stock market decline or the best solution for curbing inflation.

Laissez-faire economics

The first, and for a long time the only, widely accepted economic theory was the *laissez-faire* theory proposed by Adam Smith in his *Wealth of Nations* (1776). *Laissez-faire* roughly translates as "to leave alone," and it means that government should not interfere in the economy. This theory favors low taxes and free trade, and it strongly holds that the market is self-adjusting—whatever happens will be corrected over time without the help of the government.

Keynesian economic theory

John Maynard Keynes, an English economist, published his *General Theory of Employment, Interest, and Money* (1936) during the Depression. He argued that government should manipulate the economy to reverse the periodic downturns that take place in the market.

Keynes maintained that economic depression was due to a lack of consumer demand. This created excess inventories of goods that forced business to cut production and lay off workers, which led to fewer consumers and even lower demand. The solution was to increase demand by increasing government spending and cutting taxes. This **fiscal policy,** as it became known, left people with more money after taxes and basic obligations to use for goods and services. Factories increased production to meet the demand and hired more workers.

Franklin Roosevelt used many of Keynes's ideas in the New Deal. The federal government became the "employer of last resort" through such programs as the Civilian Conservation Corps (CCC) and the Works Progress Administration (WPA). These programs did not bring the country out of the Depression, however. The end to the Depression is more attributable to increased defense spending as World War II approached.

Monetarism

In the late 1970s and early 1980s, Keynesian economics fell into disrepute because it did not offer a solution for dealing with unemployment and inflation at the same time. Some economists argued the Keynesian theory invited excessive government intervention. To monetarists, inflation, unemployment, and stagnation were caused by policies that adversely affected an otherwise stable economy. Led by economist Milton Friedman, they argued that the best way to create a healthy economy is to control the supply of money. The machinery to implement this policy already existed in the **Federal Reserve system**, which was established in 1913.

The Federal Reserve system consists of 12 banks under a board of governors whose members serve staggered 14-year terms. This long term frees the board from the political influence of any one administration. The Federal Reserve Board controls the supply of money by buying and selling federal government securities, regulating how much money Federal Reserve banks have on deposit, and setting interest rates that member banks pay when they borrow from the Federal Reserve. The purpose is either to stimulate the economy by loosening the money supply or cool it down by tightening the money supply. In other words, the "Fed" lowers interest rates when the economy is sluggish and raises rates when inflation threatens.

Supply-side economics

Another economic problem of the late 1970s was exploding budget deficits. Because the budget is part of fiscal policy, not monetary policy, monetarism did not speak to this problem directly. Another group, called supply-side economists, offered the surprising suggestion that government could raise more money by *cutting* taxes. Their argument was fairly straightforward: High taxes were limiting national productivity, so lowering taxes would stimulate economic growth and eventually produce more revenue. The Reagan administration accepted this approach, so much so that supply-side economics became *Reaganomics.*

Two problems compromised the success of supply-side policies. The Reagan administration increased defense spending dramatically (something the theory did not take into account). Increased expenses combined with the tax cuts to produce a massive budget deficit. Moreover, much of the economic windfall went to buy products manufactured in foreign countries, and so provided little direct stimulus to the U.S. economy. Budget deficits grew even more, and unemployment remained (at least temporarily) high.

The Federal Budget

The expenses of the operations and services provided by the federal government as well as the revenues to pay for those expenses make up the federal budget. Each government program, agency, and activity receives a certain amount of money; programs with a higher priority receive more funding than those considered less important. Preparing the budget and getting it through Congress is a complicated and, needless to say, very political process. The fights between Congress and the White House over spending priorities are annual events.

Preparing the budget

Since the Budget and Accounting Act of 1921, the president has had the authority to prepare the budget each year. The **Office of Management and Budget (OMB),** which was created in 1970 in the Executive Office of the White House, advises the president on budget policy and collects and analyzes the requests for funding from all government departments and agencies. The OMB then puts the budget together based on anticipated revenues and expenditures, and it is submitted to Congress in January.

Congress's role in determining budget policy increased with the passage of the Budget and Impoundment Control Act of 1974. The legislation set up budget committees in both the House and Senate, established the **Congressional Budget Office (CBO)** to give Congress access to expert advice to conduct a comprehensive budget review, and set a timetable for approval of the budget.

Balancing the budget

Debts and deficits are not the same thing. A *deficit* occurs when, in any given time period, spending exceeds revenue. A *debt,* on the other hand, is just the total amount one owes. So it is possible to run up a deficit in one year without going into debt, as long as excess money is available to cover the shortfall. And one can run up a *surplus,* and take in more revenue than gets spent, without necessarily erasing a large debt.

Individuals and families usually cannot run up deficits for long. They quickly become buried in debt and find themselves unable to borrow more money. A national government, by contrast, can support deficit spending for many years. Creditors trust that the government will pay back loans as promised, because declaring bankruptcy would exact severe costs to both the economy and to national prestige. U.S. deficit spending increased sharply in the 1980s through a combination of tax cuts and high defense expenditures, but the borrowing was able to continue for many years.

However, even governments eventually must balance their budgets. Too much debt requires exorbitant interest payments from the national treasury and can lower economic efficiency. By the mid-1980s, American leaders became worried about the mounting debt and set out to get deficit spending under control. In response, Congress passed the Balanced Budget and Emergency Deficit Control Act (1985), better known as the **Gramm-Rudman-Hollings Bill** after its sponsors, which was intended to reduce the deficit by automatic spending cuts. Its effectiveness was reduced by excluding entitlement programs such as Social Security and Medicare from the cuts. Subsequent amendments delayed the deadline for achieving a balanced budget.

The inability of Congress and the president to work out an effective approach to the budget convinced many that the only way to achieve a balanced budget was through a constitutional amendment. Even after

Republicans gained control of Congress in 1994, a House proposal for the amendment failed in the Senate. Americans recognize that the budget process needs reform, and they support a balanced budget amendment; however, most Americans are opposed to cuts in entitlements, which make up a significant slice of the budget pie. Nevertheless, President Clinton and the Republican Congress were able to balance the budget in 1997—at least on paper, and mostly because of projected economic growth—for the first time since 1951.

Taxation and Spending

Most people want the government to do something for them, whether it's agricultural price supports, veterans' benefits, or Medicare. None of these things are free, and the government taxes its citizens to raise the money to pay for the programs. Until 1913, the revenue of the federal government came mainly from protective **tariffs,** which are taxes on goods imported into the country, and from the sale of public lands. But the tariff policy caused high prices, and the federal graduated income tax was instituted through the Sixteenth Amendment to make up for receipts lost when goods were too expensive to purchase.

Types of taxes

Many policy analysts believe that one purpose of government is to redistribute wealth. The terms used to describe methods of taxation reflect these values. Taxes that place a heavier burden on the wealthy are called **progressive taxes.** One example is the income tax, which (at least in theory) imposes a higher tax rate on those making more money. Property, inheritance, and capital gains taxes are also usually progressive. Many voluntary taxes are **regressive taxes,** which is to say the poor provide government with a disproportionate share of the revenue. Examples include gasoline taxes, as well as **sin taxes** such as those on liquor, cigarettes, and gambling. Some taxes are neutral, hitting everyone equally—such as the sales tax, in which everyone pays the same tax percentage when buying a product. Nevertheless, analysts usually call the sales tax regressive, in part because it does not "steal from the rich and give to the poor," and in part because a larger share of income goes toward necessary purchases for a working-class family than for a rich one.

Tax-reform efforts

Not paying taxes is illegal, but the government offers numerous **loopholes** that individuals and corporations may use to reduce their tax burden legally. Although the technical details can be quite complicated, the basic idea is simple: The government gives tax breaks to individuals and companies who act in a manner that policymakers want to encourage, such as buying a home, adding equipment in a factory, placing kids in child care, or entertaining clients at restaurants and sporting events. In the early 1980s, these tax deductions were sometimes so generous that large corporations did not pay any income taxes at all, leading some to conclude that the income tax system was not progressive so much as haphazard.

Proposals for tax reform include closing loopholes, simplifying tax filing, and changing tax rates. Under the 1986 Tax Reform Act, the number of tax categories was reduced, rates were lowered, and many allowable deductions were eliminated. These changes did not work as planned. Incoming tax revenue proved much less than first estimated under the law, and President George Bush was unable to keep his "no new taxes" pledge, which became a factor in his defeat in 1992. Under President Bill Clinton, tax rates were lowered for the poorest Americans and raised for the wealthy to make the system more progressive.

In addition to tinkering with the tax rates or eliminating loopholes, there have been calls for radical changes in the tax code. One proposal is the flat tax, which Steve Forbes made the basis for his campaign in the 1996 Republican primaries. A **flat tax** is a single low rate for all Americans, irrespective of income, coupled with an elimination of all exemptions. Adoption of the flat tax, proponents claim, would allow individuals to file their taxes on a post card and eliminate the need for the Internal Revenue Service. A **value-added tax (VAT),** effectively a national sales tax, would tax an item at each stage of its production. Conservatives have long argued for ending or significantly reducing the **capital gains tax,** which is a tax on income from the sale of real estate or stock. The argument here is that taxpayers would reinvest the savings, providing funds for economic expansion.

International Economic Policy

The United States is part of a global economy. We buy goods from and sell goods to other countries. Foreign companies operate here, and American firms have operations overseas. The U.S. position on questions of trade, finance, and monetary policy are important to institutions like the United Nations' **World Bank** and **International Monetary Fund (IMF).** The World Bank provides loans and technology assistance for economic development projects in member states, and the IMF seeks to promote international monetary cooperation, currency stability, and international trade.

In recent years, the principal international economic issue for the United States has been trade. The U.S. has helped negotiate many different sorts of trade agreements over the years, to ensure continued access to foreign goods and open markets abroad for goods manufactured in the U.S. The General Agreement of Tariffs and Trade (GATT), for example, was created after World War II to provide a forum for negotiating international agreements based on free trade principles. It has been superseded by the **World Trade Organization (WTO).** Through these negotiations, the United States has not only tried to keep foreign markets open but also to ensure that other countries respect patents on American products.

The **North American Free Trade Agreement (NAFTA),** which Congress ratified in 1993, established a free-trade zone between the United States, Canada, and Mexico. The agreement triggered a major public debate in the United States over its benefits and drawbacks. Organized labor strongly opposed NAFTA, arguing that Mexico's extremely low wages would encourage manufacturers to move their plants to the other side of the border. There were also concerns about the effectiveness of Mexican environmental control and occupational safety laws. H. Ross Perot made opposition to NAFTA the cornerstone of his independent run for the White House in 1992, as did Pat Buchanan in later presidential campaigns. But American policy leaders in both major parties still appear committed to free-trade principles.

Chapter Checkout

Q&A

1. Which of the following organizations provides loans and technology assistance to poor countries?

   a. World Bank
   b. International Monetary Fund
   c. World Trade Organization
   d. NAFTA

2. True or False: One important goal of economic policy is to reduce the unemployment rate to 0 percent, so that everyone in the labor force has a job.

3. Keynesian economists believe that the national government can improve economic performance by manipulating _____ policy.

4. The U.S. budget primarily came from _____ _____ before 1913, but these taxes increased the cost of imported goods too much.

Answers: 1. a 2. F (no absolute full employment) 3. fiscal 4. protective tariffs

Chapter 16

FOREIGN POLICY

Chapter Check-In

❑ Surveying the history of American foreign policy

❑ Contrasting the roles played by different policymakers

❑ Comprehending today's critical foreign-policy issues

Actions taken by the United States to promote its national interests, security, and well-being in the world come under the heading of *foreign policy.* These actions may include measures that support a competitive economy, provide for a strong defense of the nation's borders, and encourage the ideas of peace, freedom, and democracy at home and abroad. Foreign policy may contain inherent contradictions. For example, an aggressive foreign policy with a country whose activities have been perceived as threatening to U.S. security could result in a confrontation; that might undermine freedom and democracy at home. Foreign policy is never static; it must respond to and initiate actions as circumstances change.

Background of American Foreign Policy

In his farewell address, George Washington warned the United States to steer clear of foreign entanglements. From the conclusion of the War of 1812 to the Spanish-American War (1898), this advice was largely followed. American foreign policy was **isolationist;** that is, U.S. leaders saw little reason to get involved in world affairs, particularly outside the Western Hemisphere. The **Monroe Doctrine** (1823) stated that the United States would not interfere in European affairs and it would oppose any European attempt to colonize the Americas. The second part of the doctrine was effectively enforced because it reflected British desires as well. American energies were applied to settling the continent under the banner of **manifest destiny.**

The Spanish–American War and its aftermath

The Spanish-American War marked the emergence of the United States as a world power. As a result, Guam, Puerto Rico, and the Philippines became American territories; the Hawaiian Islands were annexed separately. A few years later, President Theodore Roosevelt intervened in Central and South America, including supporting the independence of Panama from Columbia in 1903, which led to construction of the Panama Canal. With the European powers carving out spheres of influence for themselves in China, the United States called for an **Open Door policy** that would allow all nations equal trading access.

World War I and World War II

The United States entered World War I in April 1917, after remaining neutral for three years. President Woodrow Wilson, who hoped his **Fourteen Points** (1918) would become the basis for the postwar settlement, played an active role in the Paris Peace Conference. The Republican-controlled Senate, however, refused to ratify the Treaty of Versailles, which provided for the creation of the League of Nations. The United States returned to isolationism during the interwar period and never joined the League. In response to the growing threat from Nazi Germany, Congress passed a series of neutrality acts (1935–1937) that were intended to keep the United States out of a European conflict. It was only after the outbreak of World War II (September 1939) that President Franklin Roosevelt was able to shift American foreign policy to aid the Allies.

With the Japanese attack on Pearl Harbor (December 7, 1941), the United States formally joined the Grand Alliance that included Great Britain, free France, the Soviet Union, and China. During the war, the Allied leaders met on several occasions to plan military strategy and to discuss the structure of the postwar world. The important wartime conferences were Casablanca (January 1943), Teheran (November 1943), Yalta (February 1945), and Potsdam (July–August 1945). Although the status of Eastern Europe was one of the main topics at Yalta and Potsdam, the fate of these countries was not determined by diplomacy but by the facts on the ground. At the end of the war, Soviet troops were in control of most of Eastern Europe behind what Winston Churchill would later call the **Iron Curtain.**

The Cold War and Vietnam

The American response to the expansion of communism and the influence of the Soviet Union was the **containment policy.** The term was coined by State Department staffer George Kennan and was based on the premise that the United States must apply counterforce to any aggressive moves by the Soviet Union. This policy was reflected in the creation of a network of political and military alliances, such as the North Atlantic Treaty

Organization (NATO), Southeast Asia Treaty Organization (SEATO), and the Central Treaty Organization (CENTO). Both the **Truman Doctrine** (1947), which committed the United States to protect "free peoples" in Europe from attack, and the **Korean War** (1950–1953) are examples of containment in practice. American policy also recognized the importance of economic assistance to prevent communism from gaining support. Under the **Marshall Plan,** named for Secretary of State George C. Marshall, the United States pumped billions of dollars into Western Europe to help with reconstruction after World War II. *Foreign aid,* direct financial aid to countries around the world for both economic and military development, became a key element of American diplomacy.

U.S. foreign policy was also guided by the **domino theory,** the thought that if one country in a region came under communist control, other nations in the area would soon follow. It was the reason the United States became involved in Vietnam, which ultimately cost 58,000 American lives, many billions of dollars, and a bitterly divided country.

The Cold War was punctuated by periods of thaw in U.S.-Soviet relations. Presidents Eisenhower, Kennedy, and Johnson met with the leaders of the Soviet Union in what was known as *summit diplomacy.* The 1963 Nuclear Test Ban Treaty, which was negotiated in the aftermath of the Cuban Missile Crisis (October 1962), was one of the positive results of these meetings.

Détente and the end of the Cold War

American foreign policy took a new direction during the 1970s. Under President Richard Nixon, **détente,** an easing of tensions between the United States and the Soviet Union, led to increased trade and cultural exchanges and, most important, to an agreement to limit nuclear weapons—the 1972 Strategic Arms Limitation Treaty (SALT I). In the same year, Nixon began the process of normalizing relations with the People's Republic of China.

Superpower rivalry continued for a time, however. The Soviet Union's invasion of Afghanistan resulted in an American-led boycott of the 1980 Moscow Olympics. President Reagan actively supported anti-communist, anti–left-wing forces in both Nicaragua and El Salvador, which he considered client states of the Soviet Union (the "evil empire"). He increased American defense spending significantly during his first term. The Soviet Union simply could not match these expenditures. Faced with a serious economic crisis, Soviet leader Mikhail Gorbachev instituted new policies called **glasnost** (openness) and **perestroika** (economic restructuring) that eased tensions with the United States. By the early 1990s, the Cold War had effectively come to an end. The Soviet Union ceased to exist with the independence of the Baltic States (Estonia, Latvia, and Lithuania), Ukraine, Belarus, Armenia, Georgia, and the Central Asian republics.

The new world order

While significantly reducing the threat of nuclear war, the collapse of the Soviet Union did not mean an end to conflict around the world. The Iraqi invasion of Kuwait in 1990 prompted the United States to put together an international coalition under the auspices of the United Nations (UN) that culminated in the brief Persian Gulf War in 1991. Both the UN and NATO were involved in seeking a resolution to the ethnic conflict in the former Yugoslavia; neither was very effective in controlling the excesses of the civil war or managing the frequent cease-fires.

Making Foreign Policy

Under the Constitution, both the president and Congress have a role in foreign policy. Each has been given specific powers and has assumed additional authority either through precedent or by relying on other constitutional responsibilities. Since the Vietnam War, Congress has tried to exert more influence and control over foreign policy.

The president and foreign policy

The president negotiates treaties, appoints ambassadors to represent the United States overseas, and is commander in chief of the armed forces. Throughout U.S. history, presidents have used their power as head of the military to involve the nation in numerous conflicts abroad without a formal declaration of war by Congress, and they have found other ways to get around constitutionally imposed limitations on their ability to set the direction of American foreign policy.

Even though they are effective only during the term of the president who made them, **executive agreements** negotiated with another head of state do not require Senate approval. Presidents also have access to discretionary funds that can be (and have been) used to finance both military and diplomatic initiatives. Presidents routinely rely on **special envoys,** who do not require Senate confirmation, to carry out negotiations with other countries.

Congress and foreign policy

The constitutional function of Congress is essentially to act as a check on presidential power. Only Congress can declare war, and the Senate must approve all treaties and confirm the president's nominees for ambassadorial and cabinet positions. Congress has additional authority through its appropriation and oversight functions. As must all government programs, the operations of foreign policy must be funded. Congress can cut or increase foreign aid or the budget for a defense project. It can set restrictions on the length of time American troops are deployed during an international crisis by refusing to pay for them beyond a certain date. The Foreign Affairs and Intelligence Committees of both the House and the Senate have investigated the Iran-Contra affair as well as the operations of the Central Intelligence Agency (CIA).

Congress has used its power to make laws that specifically limit the freedom of action of the president in foreign policy. The Neutrality Acts (1935–1937) are an early example. The 1973 **War Powers Act,** which was a direct response to the Vietnam War, requires that Congress be consulted whenever the president is ready to commit American troops. It puts a 60-day limit on their deployment (with an additional month for withdrawal) without further congressional approval. Vetoed by President Nixon and generally opposed by his successors, the act's effectiveness has been questioned. Still, President George Bush sought the support of Congress before the Persian Gulf War, as did President Bill Clinton to send troops to Somalia and Bosnia.

The mass media and foreign policy

The print and broadcast media, as discussed in Chapter 8, play a role in setting the foreign policy agenda for the country. Coverage of the Vietnam War is credited with bringing about the public-opinion shift in favor of withdrawal. Perhaps recalling Vietnam, the Defense Department severely restricted how the press could cover the Persian Gulf War. On the other hand, the images of starvation in Somalia and the graphic reports of "ethnic cleansing" during the civil war in Bosnia built support for American intervention in both of those countries.

The Institutions of Foreign Policy

Foreign policy is formulated and implemented within the executive branch. The principal policy institutions are the Departments of State and Defense, the National Security Council (NSC), and the CIA.

Department of State

The Department of State is most directly responsible for the conduct of foreign policy. The secretary of state is, in theory at least, the nation's chief foreign policy official. That role can be assumed by other officials in the administration. President Nixon relied much more heavily on Henry Kissinger when he served as Nixon's national security advisor than on Secretary of State William Rogers. The day-to-day diplomacy of the United States is carried out by the Foreign Service, which staffs American embassies and consulates around the world. Although many ambassadors are appointed for their political contributions rather than their knowledge of foreign affairs, the career Foreign Service officers are an invaluable source of information for policymakers.

Department of Defense

It is difficult, if not impossible, to separate the military from foreign policy. The Defense Department was created in 1949 through a consolidation of the War Department and the Department of the Navy (which included the Marine Corps), both of which were cabinet-level departments, and the U.S. Air Force. The secretary of defense can have tremendous influence on foreign policy, as did Robert McNamara, who served in the post under Presidents John Kennedy and Lyndon Johnson during the Vietnam War. The **Joint Chiefs of Staff,** who are the heads of the four branches of the armed services and a chairperson, provide advice to the president on military planning and strategy.

National Security Council

The **National Security Council (NSC)** is made up of the president and vice president, the secretaries of defense and state, the director of the CIA, the chair of the Joint Chiefs of Staff (the leadership council for the armed services), and about a dozen other government officials; it is headed by the national security advisor. The council is responsible for advising the president on foreign policy. The role of the NSC varies from administration to administration. Nixon, who was extremely knowledgeable about foreign affairs, relied on the NSC a great deal. Indeed, his national security advisor, Henry Kissinger, was intimately involved in opening relations with the People's Republic of China, and he represented the United States in the peace negotiations with North Vietnam.

Central Intelligence Agency

Created at the end of World War II, the **Central Intelligence Agency (CIA)** collects, analyzes, evaluates, and disseminates information (intelligence) relating to the national security of the United States. Although the CIA uses a variety of means to gather information, most of it comes from simply reading both official and mass-market publications from around the world. The most controversial of the agency's activities are its **covert operations,** which have involved assassination, assisting in the overthrow of a government, and tampering with elections.

Issues in Foreign Policy

For almost half a century, the main objective of American foreign policy has been to counter the threat from the Soviet Union. While national security questions and relations with Russia remain high on the foreign policy agenda, new questions have come to the fore. Increasing global interdependence in economic development, communications, and the environment is blurring the distinction between domestic and foreign policy.

National security issues

With the collapse of the Soviet Union, the pace of nuclear disarmament quickened. American and Russian nuclear missiles are no longer targeted at each other, and the United States has worked with the newly independent countries of Belarus, Ukraine, and Kazakhstan to dismantle the nuclear arsenals on their territory. Nuclear proliferation and the danger of terrorist groups or renegade states, such as Iraq, Iran, and Libya, using weapons of mass destruction (nuclear, biological, and chemical) remain major foreign policy concerns.

The concept of a "new world order" suggested that the United States would act through coalitions rather than assume the role of the world's policeman. While coalitions worked during and immediately after the Persian Gulf War, they proved less successful in Bosnia and Somalia. Indeed, it was an American initiative that brought about the tentative settlement in Bosnia through the Dayton Accords, and the United States is a critical go-between in the Arab-Israeli conflict.

Throughout the Cold War, the United States relied on NATO to check Soviet expansion in Europe. With that danger removed, a reevaluation of the role of this military alliance is taking place. One development is the interest of the countries of Eastern Europe and the former Soviet Union in becoming members of NATO.

International economic policy

As shown in the last chapter, decisions made about international economic policy have a direct domestic impact. Economic policy is also used as a tool in foreign policy. American companies are prohibited from doing business with countries that are identified as sponsors of terrorism. Working through the UN, the United States has tried to make sure that Iraq cannot sell its oil on the world market to rebuild its military strength. Economic boycotts and sanctions are employed to force other nations to alter their policy or to bring about changes in human rights.

Environmental issues

The environment is a comparatively new issue in foreign policy. The discovery of a hole in the ozone layer over Antarctica and evidence of global warming demonstrate that environmental change has a global impact and requires international action. Through international agreements, progress has been made in reducing the production of chemicals that destroy ozone. Global warming, which many scientists believe has already begun and is traceable to the burning of fossil fuels, is a more difficult problem. Strong action here would not only affect industrialized countries but would impose severe hardships on the developing countries that do not have the resources to shift to other energy sources. A related issue that was raised at the 1992 United Nations Conference on the Environment and Development (the Earth Summit) is biodiversity decline, that is, the rapidly falling number of plant and animal species in the world. The United States did not support the biodiversity treaty that came out of the conference.

Chapter Checkout

Q&A

1. Faced with a serious economic crisis, Soviet President Mikhail Gorbachev moved the globe toward its "new world order" by instituting a new openness in the USSR called

   a. perestroika

   b. glasnost

   c. détente

   d. potsdam

   e. stolichnaya

2. The Truman Doctrine and the Korean War are both examples of the United States' _____ policy, dominant in the 1950s, which stated that Soviet expansion would be met by an appropriate counter force.

3. List at least three foreign-policy actions that the president may take without seeking congressional approval.

Answers: 1. b 2. containment 3. using special envoys, making executive agreements, spending discretionary funds, deploying troops for less than two months.

CQR REVIEW

Use this CQR Review to reinforce and practice what you've learned in this book. After you work through the review questions, you're well on your way to understanding American politics and government.

Chapters 1–5

1. The Constitutional Convention of 1787 worked through a series of competing plans to resolve the debate between

   a. large state delegates vs. small state delegates.
   b. pro-slavery delegates vs. anti-slavery delegates.
   c. delegates wanting a strong national government vs. those favoring the states.
   d. those supporting Thomas Jefferson vs. those who opposed him.

2. Which of the following best describes *The Federalist Papers*?

   a. A list of the specific reasons why the American colonies wanted to separate from England
   b. James Madison's notes from the Constitutional Convention keeping track of the debates
   c. The rough draft for what eventually became the Bill of Rights
   d. A series of newspaper articles supporting the proposed U.S. Constitution

3. Which view of federalism corresponds most closely with the idea of "states' rights"?

   a. Unitary federalism
   b. Cooperative federalism
   c. Dual federalism
   d. Marble-cake federalism

4. True or False: In the Articles of Confederation, each state was represented in the Confederation Congress according to the size of its population, with Rhode Island the least influential state.

5. True or False: The U.S. Supreme Court has ruled that states may not place a legal limit on how many terms their elected congressional representatives may serve.

6. True or False: The proliferation of subcommittees in Congress has sped up the legislative process by creating groups of experts in each policy area.

7. True or False: Appointments to the Executive Office usually have closer political ties to the president than those appointed to serve as cabinet secretaries.

8. True or False: In an attempt to appear bipartisan, presidents usually alternate their Supreme Court appointments to balance between judges affiliated with the two major parties.

9. The legislative branch _____ the laws, the executive branch _____ the laws, and the judicial branch _____ the laws.

10. Gov. Elbridge Gerry signed into law an 1812 elections bill that included a salamander-shaped congressional district sure to elect Republicans to office. As a result, strategically designed election districts are now called _____s, and the act of drawing such districts is called _____ing.

11. A representative who considers it his or her job to express the direct will of voters back home is often called a _____, whereas one who emphasizes his or her own best judgment is often called a _____.

12. Congress tried to give the President a _____ veto power enjoyed by many governors, which is the capability to veto particular appropriations contained in a larger bill, but the U.S. Supreme Court declared this new delegation of authority to be unconstitutional.

13. The President may negotiate treaties and appoint judges and other important officials, but all of these actions must be approved by the _____.

14. Pick three government policies that matter to your daily life (such as education, transportation, or banking). Do they make more sense as a responsibility of local government, state government, or the national government? Can you think of different facets of those policies that make sense for different levels of government?

15. The theory of marble-cake federalism suggests that almost every public policy involves cooperation among multiple levels of government. Select a policy that interests you (such as education, transportation, or criminal justice) and investigate the distribution of responsibilities

for this effort. How much is controlled by each level of government? Is the policy really cooperative, or is it primarily dominated by one level? To research this question, look at scholarly literature, review government documents, or arrange interviews with people knowledgeable about the area.

16. Pick a single piece of legislation either narrowly passed or narrowly defeated in the last congressional session, and tell the story of this bill. Using government documents as well as news coverage, trace the passage of this bill through each stage of congressional consideration. Develop a list of the arguments made for and against the bill. Which interests supported it, and which opposed it? Keep track of the amendments considered during the process. If the House and Senate passed different versions of the bill, figure out which elements of each version emerged from the conference committee. If the bill cleared Congress but the President vetoed it, did Congress try to override the veto? If so, check to see how the vote differed the second time around.

Chapters 6–8

17. The largest administrative units in government are the

   a. government corporations.
   b. regulatory commissions.
   c. independent agencies.
   d. cabinet departments.

18. True or False: The Constitution does not allow government to ban communications based upon whether they are obscene; obscenity is protected by the First Amendment.

19. The _____ tradition of hard-hitting investigative journalism in weekly and monthly news magazines helped produced the reform movements of the Progressive Era.

20. The Supreme Court in 1971 forbid the Nixon administration's attempt to prohibit publication of the _____ Papers, a confidential assessment of the nation's Vietnam policy. The Court noted that constitutional free press guarantees did not allow _____ _____ of publications.

21. The public often gets its way on public policy, but sometimes the government ignores widely held beliefs. One instance, of course, is when the Supreme Court strikes down a popular law as unconstitutional. But thinking about what you know of Congress, the presidency, and the bureaucracy, try to come up with three or four

other reasons why a majority might be unable to impose its policy preferences on the country.

22. Watch network television for an hour and keep track of every advertisement that you see. Record the number of positive ads, negative ads, and neutral ads that appear for various products and services. Which ads are most effective at making you prefer the product of the advertiser? Which sorts of products are advertised negatively and which ones positively? Speculate on why the companies that "go negative" might have used a strategy similar to that used in political campaigns, whereas other products are sold in a different way. Are the two sorts of products different in some way, and are the products sold negatively somehow more similar to politicians?

23. Select two organizations with which you are familiar, such as a campus club, a sports team or recreational league, a religious group, or a place of employment. For each one, determine whether it meets the definition of a "bureaucracy"—that is, whether it (a) includes specialized members, (b) is organized hierarchically, and (c) follows formal rules.

Chapters 9–11

24. Third parties are not very successful in America because

   a. the proportional representation system used in the U.S. gives them too few legislative seats.

   b. they never receive enough votes to win campaign funds from the federal government.

   c. the two major parties generally ignore the issues that matter to third parties.

   d. the two major parties are subsidized by government and exclude third parties from debates.

25. The "coattails effect" refers to when a president

   a. wears stately clothing to impress foreign dignitaries and make Americans feel safe.

   b. attaches personal provisions into longer legislation so that it will get through Congress.

   c. brings close friends from a home state to Washington so they can help run the show.

   d. pulls members of the same party into Congress at a high rate during an election.

26. In many European countries, minor parties are more likely to have members serving in the legislative branch, because legislators are elected using a system of _____ representation.

27. Voters who cannot vote in their home county may request a/an _____ ballot.

28. The party of the president almost always loses congressional seats in _____ elections, although President Bill Clinton and the Democrats bucked this trend in 1998.

29. True or False: Industries such as banking and telecommunications typically are governed by an "iron triangle" of lobbyists, bureaucrats, and congressional committee members.

Chapters 12–13

30. True or False: The Social Security trust fund was running out of money until payroll taxes increased in the early 1980s.

31. True or False: The first eight constitutional amendments apply to the states, not just the federal government, because they have been incorporated through the Fourteenth Amendment due process clause.

32. True or False: Because the Supreme Court demanded in 1954 that schools integrate "with all deliberate speed," Southern leaders knew that they could comply with the demand slowly.

33. More than 50 percent of the federal budget is dedicated toward _____ such as Social Security and Medicare, expenditures that are promised to individuals meeting particular criteria.

34. Set up an interview with a small businessperson, say someone who hires between two and 30 regular employees. Ask them about the governmental regulations with which they must comply. Depending upon how specific your source is willing to be, try to get a cost estimate for these regulations. Then select two or three of the regulations you were told about. Research these rules: who imposed them, why were they imposed. Finally, draw a conclusion: Based upon the costs and benefits of the regulations, do you think they were a good idea or a poor one?

Chapters 14–16

35. Which economic theory proposes that the federal government can improve the nation's economic performance by manipulating fiscal policy?

   a. Laissez-faire economics
   b. Keynesian economics
   c. Monetarism
   d. Supply-side economics

36. True or False: Most economists now believe that President Franklin Roosevelt's Keynesian domestic policy initiatives were responsible for pulling the United States out of the Great Depression.

37. True or False: The U.S. took its first major step toward being a global power when President Woodrow Wilson, with the advice and consent of the Senate, accepted the Treaty of Versailles and enrolled the country in the League of Nations.

38. When government spending exceeds government revenue, it's called a _____. Too many years of this can produce a large _____.

Answers: 1. a **2.** d **3.** c **4.** F **5.** T **6.** F **7.** T **8.** F **9.** Makes, carries out, interprets **10.** Gerrymander **11.** Delegate, trustee **12.** Line-item **13.** Senate **14.** Provide your own answer **15.** Provide your own answer **16.** Provide your own answer **17.** d **18.** F **19.** Muckraker **20.** Pentagon, prior restraint **21.** Provide your own answer **22.** Provide your own answer **23.** Provide your own answer **24.** d **25.** d **26.** Proportional **27.** Absentee **28.** Midterm **29.** F **30.** F **31.** F **32.** T **33.** Entitlements **34.** Provide your own answer **35.** b **36.** F **37.** F **38.** Deficit, debt

CQR RESOURCE CENTER

CQR Resource Center offers the best resources available in print and online to help you study and review the core concepts of American government and politics. You can find additional resources, plus study tips and tools to help test your knowledge, at www.cliffsnotes.com.

Books

This CliffsQuickReview book is one of many great books about American government and politics. If you want some additional resources, check out these other publications:

Politics For Dummies, by Ann Delaney, takes readers of all ages through the murky political waters of the U.S. with just enough wit to make it all interesting. Delaney's book helps take the fear out of politics. Hungry Minds, Inc. $19.99.

The New American Democracy, by Morris Fiorina and Paul Peterson, is one of the best new textbooks on American politics. The book offers a challenging argument: that elections drive American politics today more than they have at any earlier time in U.S. history, and more than is true in other industrialized democracies. An Essentials edition, more book than textbook, is also forthcoming from Penguin. Longman Alternate Edition. $60.00.

Politics by Other Means, by Benjamin Ginsberg and Martin Shefter, offers a much more skeptical view of elections. They say that Americans seldom solve their differences through the electoral process anymore, instead turning to tactics such as lawsuits and protests. W.W. Norton. $15.00

America the Unusual, by John Kingdon, offers a detailed comparison between the U.S. government and the governments found in other industrialized democracies to show that American really is exceptional. The differences between the U.S. and other nations comes down to one fact, an abiding belief in limited government, that shows up across the government's ideologies, institutions, and policies. St. Martin's/WORTH. $21.00.

Only in America?, by Graham Wilson, challenges the view that America is exceptional. Certainly American government has always been more limited than that found in similar nations, but the government has been growing in most countries, and the U.S. has kept pace. Chatham House. $21.95.

Hungry Minds also has three Web sites that you can visit to read about all the books we publish:

- www.cliffsnotes.com
- www.dummies.com
- www.hungryminds.com

Internet

Visit the following Web sites for more information about American government:

Yahoo Search Engine, www.yahoo.com, includes a pointer to the Web pages of most major news outlets. From the index page, you can click on News and Media, then Newspapers, to find the Web pages of *The New York Times, Washington Post, USA Today,* and other papers that maintain politics pages.

Poly-Cy, www.polsci.wvu.edu/polycy/, is a reference page for people interested in political science (rather than just politics). It points users to the main journals, professional associations, and research sites.

Project Vote-Smart, www.vote-smart.org/, is a group dedicated to stripping the nonsense from American politics to focus on issues. Board members from across the political spectrum add an air of nonpartisanship to this information source, which focuses on political campaigns.

The National Election Studies, www.umich.edu/~nes/, offers the most commonly used data in political science for studying elections. The NES schedules a major academic survey of American voters for every U.S. election, probing people's political views to make voting behavior more understandable.

The Federal Elections Project, www.american.edu/academic. depts/spa/ccps/elections/, is collecting year 2000 precinct-level voting data from every state in the United States and linking the data as much as possible to results of the last census. These election returns are useful for studying all sorts of ideas about voting in the U.S. and would be particularly valuable to students writing term papers in upper-level American government classes.

Next time you're on the Internet, don't forget to drop by www. cliffsnotes.com.

GLOSSARY

absentee ballot   Used to allow people to vote when they are traveling or living away from their normal residence.

affirmative action   Policies that favor members of a protected group; used to equalize conditions in society.

American Independent party   Political party whose most famous presidential candidate was Alabama governor George Wallace; mainly known for opposing racial desegregation.

American Indian Movement (AIM)   Interest group that helps Native American tribes press land claims.

American party   Anti-immigration party dominant in the 1850s. Also called the *Know-Nothing party.*

Americans with Disabilities Act of 1990 (ADA)   Applied portions of the 1964 Civil Rights Act to the handicapped, resulting in lawsuits and institutional expenditures to increase access for the disabled.

amicus curiae brief   Written arguments in which a "friend of the court" states its position on a case.

Annapolis Convention   Gathering of representatives from five U.S. states that first formally discussed strengthening the U.S. Confederation dramatically; met in 1786 and led the way to the U.S. Constitution.

Antifederalists   Leaders in the debate over ratification who opposed the Federalists; often wanted to protect the power of state governments and therefore opposed the proposed Constitution.

Articles of Confederation   Created as a charter for the United States and in effect 1781–1787; essentially a loose alliance of sovereign states. Replaced by the Constitution.

bicameral   A legislature with two chambers.

bipartisan   Issues that unite people in both major parties.

black codes   Restrictions placed upon African-American freemen in the aftermath of their emancipation.

Black Muslims   Radical African-American religious group advocating some racial separation and threatening violence to white society.

Black Panther party   Militant African-American organization willing to use violence to increase "black power."

block grant   General federal grants for whole areas of public policy; gives the recipient flexibility.

broadcast media   Journalistic outlets that communicate using the airwaves (radio, television).

Bull-Moose party   Short-lived political party that served as a vehicle for Teddy Roosevelt's 1912 campaign for president.

bureaucrats   Employees of government agencies.

cabinet   A collection of federal department heads that reports directly to the president.

cabinet departments Administrative units in the federal bureaucracy with responsibility for broad areas of government operation.

capital gains tax Tax on the income made from sales of real estate or stock.

categorical grant Federal funds available to states and localities earmarked for a specific purpose.

caucus State gathering of political party members to select candidates for office.

Central Intelligence Agency Collects and analyzes information relevant to the national security of the U.S.

checks and balances System in which each branch of government has the ability to limit powers possessed by other branches.

chief clerk model Approach to the presidency in which the executive branch is merely an administrative arm of Congress.

chief of staff The president's main legislative liaison and staff organizer.

circuit The geographical area covered by a federal court of appeal.

civil cases Court cases in which the plaintiff tries to recover damages for something done to them by the defendant, as opposed to criminal cases.

civil disobedience When activists break a law that they consider unjust as a public challenge to the law.

civil liberties Individual freedoms on which the government may not infringe.

Civil Rights Act of 1964 Expansive federal law that prevented racial discrimination by any private business

receiving federal money or engaging in commerce with an interstate component.

Civil Rights Act of 1968 Banned discrimination in housing.

civil rights Treatment guaranteed to individuals by the government; necessary if everyone is to be equal before the law.

civil service Civilian employees of the federal government who do not lose their jobs when political control of the government changes. Also called "civil servants."

class-action suits When a group of people joins litigation against a single defendant for damages imposed on members of the group.

clear and present danger Standard used to judge speech restrictions that are allowed only when an exercise of free speech would directly threaten public safety.

closed primary Primary election in which only a party's registered voters may help select a party's candidate in the general election.

cloture A vote of 60 or more Senators, required to end a filibuster.

coattails effect The ability of a presidential candidate to pull members of the same party into Congress.

COLAs Cost of living adjustments guaranteeing that government benefits increase with the inflation rate; generally in place for program to help the elderly but not those to help families, children, or students.

commerce clause Constitutional provision giving Congress authority to regulate interstate commerce.

community standard When the definition of obscenity shifts depending on the values of a locale.

compensatory damages Direct payback sought to recover from damages caused by a defendant.

Compromise of 1850 Second great compromise between Northern and Southern states over the slavery issue; resulted in the admission of California as a free state and a fugitive slave law protecting the South.

concurring opinion Opinion written by a court minority that accepts the judgment but for alternative reasoning.

confederation System of government in which decentralized units, such as states, are clearly dominant.

conference committees Legislative committees that reconcile the discrepancies in versions of a bill passed by each chamber.

confirmation When the Senate approves a presidential appointee.

Congressional Budget Office (CBO) Office of budgetary experts that provides Congress with estimates of how much money programs will cost and taxes will provide.

congressional campaign committee Organization responsible for helping their party retain seats in, and gain new seats to, a particular chamber of Congress.

Connecticut Compromise See *Great Compromise.*

constituents The voters that any particular elected official represents.

constitutional interpretation When a court must interpret the meaning of laws written into a constitution.

containment policy American policy to resist the spread of communism through counterforce.

cooperative federalism Federal system in which different levels of government divide responsibility for public policy areas.

Copperheads Northern Democrats who opposed the nation's Civil War.

cost-benefit analysis When decision-makers weigh the costs and benefits of a public policy to decide whether it should be continued or changed.

covert operations Secret foreign policy actions intended to promote American interests abroad; can include assassination, the overthrow of foreign governments, and tampering with elections.

cozy triangle See *iron triangle.*

criminal cases Court cases in which someone is accused of damaging society through their unlawful acts, as opposed to civil cases.

de facto segregation Racial separation that comes about as a result of private social practices.

de jure segregation Racial separation enforced by law.

defendant Person charged with a crime.

delegated powers See *enumerated powers.*

delegates People at a national party convention with the power to help select candidates for office; representatives who see their job as giving the majority what it wants.

deregulation Movement to reduce the quantity of rules imposed on industries by the federal government.

desegregation The removal of laws that keep two ethnic groups apart.

détente American policy in the 1970s to ease tensions with the Soviet Union.

direct mail Mailings by candidates or interest groups targeted at individuals likely to give them money or to join their campaign.

dissenting opinion Opinion written by a court minority that rejects both the court's decision and its reasoning.

divided government When different political parties control different branches of government.

docket The Supreme Court's agenda of which cases it will hear.

domino theory The belief that allowing a single country to become Communist would result in many more countries in the region to do the same.

double jeopardy When a person is tried twice for the same crime; forbidden by the Fifth Amendment.

dual federalism Federal system in which national powers and state powers are sharply differentiated.

due process Violations of due process are forbidden by the Fifth Amendment; however, judges disagree over whether this is merely a procedural guarantee or whether it actually rules out specific governmental actions (that is, substantive due process).

elastic clause See *necessary and proper clause.*

Electoral College Indirect system for electing the U.S. President. Means that the winning candidate may not have received a majority of votes nationwide.

eminent domain Fifth Amendment requirement that government compensates owners appropriately when taking private property for public use.

entitlements Benefits promised by law to individuals or families meeting certain requirements.

enumerated powers Specific list of Congressional powers included in Article I of the Constitution; system in which a constitution lists what a limited government is allowed to do.

Equal Rights Amendment (ERA) Proposed constitutional amendment that promised women equal rights; narrowly missed ratification; amendments to the Civil Rights Act have probably produced the same effect its ratification would have had.

equal time rule Requires that radio and television stations allow candidates for political office equal access to airtime.

equality of opportunity When everyone is given the same chances to succeed by public policy but the law does not guarantee that everyone will be equal.

equality of outcome When a law is less concerned with fair or equal treatment and is more concerned with minimizing differences between groups or people at the end of the process.

exclusionary rule Courtroom ban on evidence obtained improperly.

executive agreements Presidential promises to other nations that do not require Senate approval; not binding on future administrations.

exit polls Polls taken during an election as voters leave the polling place; used to determine likely election results quickly.

fairness doctrine   Policy that required broadcasters to present all points of view on important public issues; abolished in 1987.

Federal Communications Commission   Government agency responsible for regulating the public airwaves.

Federal Election Campaign Act   Passed in 1971 and subsequently amended, this law limited how much money individuals and organizations could give to candidates for national office.

Federal Election Commission   Created in 1974, this agency monitors national elections and provides matching funds to qualifying candidates.

Federal Reserve system   The national government's banking system used to implement monetary policy.

federalism   Division of power between the national and state governments, with each one having responsibility over the tasks best performed at that level.

Federalists   Leaders in the debate over ratification who favored a strong national government and therefore supported the proposed Constitution.

The Federalist Papers   Series of newspaper articles published in New York state by Publius (the pseudonym used by Alexander Hamilton, James Madison, and John Jay). Provided numerous arguments in favor of the proposed U.S. Constitution.

fighting words   Words that most people would expect to produce violence if directed at a particular individual or group.

filibuster   When Senators delay a bill by giving marathon speeches; only stopped with a cloture vote.

First Continental Congress   Gathering of colonial representatives in 1774 that sought a peaceful settlement with Great Britain.

fiscal policy   When government tries to manipulate the economy using its tax-and-spend powers.

flat tax   A single tax imposed equally on every American that would replace income taxes and eliminate the need for the Internal Revenue Service.

formula grant   Categorical grants awarded to states and municipalities in which the amount is determined by plugging statistics into a specific formula.

Fourteen Points   President Woodrow Wilson's proposal for a peace settlement after World War I.

franchise   The right to vote.

franking privilege   Free use of the mail provided to incumbent legislators so that they may keep in touch with their constituents.

free-rider problem   The difficulty faced by interest groups when trying to attract members who will benefit from their activities even when they do not contribute.

gender gap   An abiding difference noted between men and unmarried women in their partisanship and political ideologies.

gerrymandering   The design of oddly shaped legislative districts to ensure victory by a particular party or ethnic group.

glasnost   Policy of "openness" introduced by Soviet leader Mikhail Gorbachev to ease tensions with the United States.

good faith exception Relative permission rule used to determine which evidence may be used in a criminal trial, giving police more flexibility.

government corporations Federal agencies that operate like private businesses to provide specific services.

Gramm-Rudman-Hollings bill Unsuccessful law, passed in 1985, that was supposed to eliminate the federal government's large deficits.

grand jury Method of determining whether the government should prosecute a criminal case; required in serious cases by the Fifth Amendment.

Great Compromise Settled the Constitutional Convention's debate over representation; featured a bicameral legislature, with a Senate favoring small states and a House of Representatives favoring large states. Also called the *Connecticut Compromise.*

Great Society Ambitious liberal vision pursued by President Lyndon Johnson in the 1960s.

Green party Recent, European-style political party that supports strong environmental laws and increased avenues for public participation in government.

gross national product (GNP) A measure of the nation's overall economic productivity.

Hatch Act Passed in 1939; prohibits federal workers from engaging in political activity.

ideological interest groups Interest groups that evaluate multiple policy areas based upon a coherent political ideology.

International Monetary Fund (IMF) Promotes currency stability and international trade.

impeachment Bringing a public official up on formal charges. In the federal government, impeachment is the job of the House of Representatives.

implementation When the federal bureaucracy puts federal rules and regulations into practice.

incumbents Candidates seeking to keep a position that they already hold.

independent agencies Federal agencies outside the cabinet structure that are insulated from political interference.

inflation Price increases that reduce the value of money and indirectly "tax" people with fixed incomes or property.

infomercial A long advertisement that digs into the details of a product or candidate.

initiative When voters decide policy after an issue is placed on the ballot by citizen petition.

integration Active legal measures intended to bring two ethnic groups together.

Iron Curtain The string of Eastern European nations taken over by the Soviet Union after World War II to form a barrier against the European democracies.

iron triangle A small group of people controlling a particular policy area; includes select members of congressional committees, administrative agencies, and lobbying groups. Also called a *cozy triangle.*

isolationist Term describing a passive foreign policy that does not permit getting involved in international disputes or other nations' internal affairs.

issue network More open than an iron triangle; the complex web of individuals who shape a policy area in the modern American political system.

Jim Crow Laws Southern statutes passed around the turn of the 20th century setting up a rigid racial-caste system.

Joint Chiefs of Staff Consists of a leader representing each branch of the armed services; provides the president with military advice.

joint committees Legislative committees with members drawn from both chambers; responsible for investigating issues of general concern to the Congress.

judicial activism When judges aggressively apply their judicial review power to strike down laws, as a means of making policy conform to their own preferences.

judicial restraint When judges strike down laws only rarely, otherwise deferring to the policy choices of legislatures.

judicial review The power of a court to strike down laws as unconstitutional.

Know-Nothing party See *American party.*

Korean War Early 1950s conflict in which the U.S. joined South Korea against Communist North Korea.

laissez-faire A belief that government should stay out of most areas in American life.

land-grant colleges Agricultural and mechanical colleges created under the auspices of the Morrill Act.

leadership model Approach to the presidency in which the executive branch is a competing political institution with Congress.

leaks Unauthorized releases of information to the press, sometimes used strategically to influence policy.

Lemon test Test derived from a 1971 Supreme Court ruling to determine whether a law constitutes an establishment of religion.

libel Untrue statements harmful to a person's reputation that are communicated in print.

Libertarian party Political party active since the 1960s that opposes government activity beyond police powers and the court system.

libertarianism Also known as classical liberalism; an ideology favoring limited government in both economic and social spheres.

line-item veto When an executive may cut out specific spending provisions from a larger bill.

litmus tests When voters decide whom to support based upon their positions on one or two issues.

lobbyists Paid professionals who try to influence legislation.

logrolling Cooperative effort of multiple legislators to bind together a series of personal projects and push them through the legislative process.

loopholes Specific tax provisions that allow individuals or corporations to get out of part of their tax burden by engaging in actions favored by the government.

majority floor leader Second in command of the House of Representatives.

majority opinion Opinion summarizing a court's judgment and reasoning when a court majority is in agreement.

mandate Federal regulations to which states and municipalities must adhere. Also, when the vote in a particular election implicitly endorses the views espoused by a candidate ahead of time.

manifest destiny The belief that the U.S. was destined to spread across the North American continent to the Pacific Ocean.

margin of error The amount that a poll result will fluctuate if the method is used repeatedly.

Marshall Plan U.S. program after World War II to build up Western Europe by giving war-torn nations billions of dollars.

McCulloch v. Maryland Supreme Court ruling of 1819 that used the elastic clause to justify a national bank.

Medicaid Program providing medical benefits to the poor.

Medicare Program providing medical benefits to the elderly; an immense and growing portion of the federal budget.

midterm elections Congressional elections held in years without a presidential contest.

minority floor leader Chief spokesperson and legislative strategist for the minority party in the House of Representatives.

Miranda warning Speech given by police to suspects upon making an arrest; informs suspects of their constitutional rights.

Missouri Compromise Deal negotiated in 1820 by Kentuckian Henry Clay to prevent a clash between Northern and Southern states over the slavery issue; required that the nation admit states in pairs, one slave and one free.

Monroe Doctrine Formulated in 1823, promised that the U.S. would stay out of European affairs but would oppose European attempts to colonize the Americas.

muckrakers Critical investigative journalists especially active at exposing corruption during the Progressive Era.

National Security Council Large foreign policy council responsible for advising the president on foreign policy.

natural rights Fundamental limits on what government can take away from individuals.

necessary and proper clause Constitutional provision giving Congress the right to make all laws "necessary and proper" to put its powers into effect. Used to justify wide expansion of government authority. Also called the *elastic clause.*

negative advertising Campaign ads that criticize an opponent rather than promote a candidate.

New Federalism Nixon's attempt to return authority to the states.

New Jersey Plan Moderate departure from the Articles of Confederation proposed as a response to the Virginia Plan; favored by smaller states.

nonpartisan Issues that have nothing to do with party politics.

nonpartisan elections Elections in which candidates cannot identify their party affiliation on the ballot.

North American Free Trade Agreement (NAFTA) Opened trade among three countries: the U.S., Canada, and Mexico.

Office of Management and Budget (OMB) Used by the president to filter proposed regulations and budgetary requests from the federal bureaucracy.

Open Door policy U.S. proposal to settle disputes over trade with China in the early 20th century; would allow the European powers and the U.S. to trade with China equally.

open elections Elections in which no candidate currently holds the office.

open primary Primary election in which independents, and sometimes also members of other parties, may help select a party's candidate in the general election.

party platform The formal statement of a political party's beliefs and goals.

patronage Jobs awarded to people for faithful political service.

Pendleton Act Passed in 1883, created the civil service system of hiring and retaining federal workers independent of their political allegiance.

Pentagon papers Classified documents detailing American policy in Vietnam; the U.S. Supreme Court did not allow the Nixon administration to censor their publication.

People's party See *Populist party.*

perestroika Policy of economic restructuring introduced by Soviet leader Mikhail Gorbachev intended to open the Soviet economy, thereby avoiding continued economic crisis.

plaintiff Person bringing a suit against a defendant.

planks Individual issue positions mentioned in a party platform.

platform See *party platform.*

plea bargain When a defendant admits to a lesser crime to avoid facing more serious charges in court.

pocket veto When the President rejects a bill by refusing to sign it after Congress has adjourned.

political action committees (PACs) Interest groups that raise and distribute money to candidates.

political machines Urban political organizations that dominated city politics by providing supporters with jobs and favorable attention from government.

Populist party Primarily rural political party active in the late 19th century that opposed Eastern corporate interests, especially the railroads. Also called the *People's party.*

populists Politicians who favor an active government to help common people.

pork-barrel legislation A bill funding improvement projects, such as highway construction.

precedent Prior body of law that must govern a court's decision in a particular case.

president of the Senate Role played by the Vice-President as the Senate's presiding officer; breaks tie votes.

president pro tempore Official who leads the Senate's day-to-day operations.

primary election Also called primaries, these contests allow voters to pick which candidate will represent a party in the general election.

print media Journalistic outlets that communicate using the printed word (newspapers, magazines).

prior restraint When government censors a message before it is communicated, rather than punishing it afterward.

probable cause Fourth Amendment limit on the conditions under which a federal judge may issue a search warrant.

Progressive party Coalition of farmers, unions, and middle-class reformers that challenged two-party dominance during the early 20th century.

progressive taxes Taxes that burden people more when they have greater income or wealth.

Prohibition party Long-lived single-issue party that opposed the consumption of alcoholic beverages.

project grant A categorical grant awarded on the basis of competitive applications to accomplish a specific task.

proportional representation A system in which parties receive seats in a legislative body roughly proportional to their share of the votes.

public interest groups Interest groups that claim to speak for the American public at large.

punitive damages Additional monetary fine imposed on a defendant to ensure that damages are not repeated.

rationality test Applied to most governmental laws that categorize people; only requires that the differential treatment have a rational basis. Not used for categorization based upon race, religion, or gender, for example.

Reapportionment Act of 1929 Fixed the House of Representatives at 435 voting members.

reapportionment The adjustment of Congressional districts that follows a federal census; intended to keep district populations balanced.

recall An election that allows voters to remove an incumbent from office.

red tape Complications and paperwork imposed on government agencies to ensure that their actions conform to the intent of a law.

referendum When a law or constitutional amendment passed by a state legislature must be approved by voters before taking effect.

Reform party Political party that regularly nominates outsiders for public office, often those dedicated to increasing public participation in government, lowering the federal budget deficit, and reducing trade with foreign countries.

regressive taxes Taxes that hit hardest on those who are less well off. Also sometimes applied to taxes that treat everyone equally.

regulation Rules placed by the federal government on how industries operate.

regulatory commissions Federal agencies with responsibility in specific areas of policy.

regulatory policy The policy setting governmental regulations. See also *regulation.*

representative sample A group selected for polling in which everyone in a population had an equal chance of being selected.

reverse discrimination   When a law or policy works so hard to protect a minority group that it unfairly penalizes members of the dominant group.

riders   Unrelated provisions stuck into a bill.

Rules Committee   Powerful House body that decides the terms under which bills are heard, amended, and debated.

runoff election   Contest in which the top two vote-getters from a previous election face off to decide the ultimate winner.

schema   A set of beliefs, or a story, applied when trying to understand a particular political event.

Second Continental Congress Assumed governmental functions in the American colonies after the battles of Lexington and Concord in 1775.

select committees   Temporary legislative committees that consider specific issues, especially to investigate problems. Also called *special committees.*

selective incorporation   The process of applying the Bill of Rights to the states selectively, based upon a judicial judgment of which rights are fundamental.

self-incrimination   When individuals testify against themselves in a court hearing; Fifth Amendment forbids forcing anyone to do this.

seniority   The number of years someone has served in an institution or on a committee.

separation of powers   Idea that different governmental powers should be placed in separate branches (or institutions) so that no one interest can monopolize governmental authority.

Shay's Rebellion   Revolt of Western Massachusetts farmers in the winter of 1786–1787, in which they demanded relief from debts.

sin taxes   Taxes imposed on products that many people consider "sinful"; intended both to discourage use of these products and to let government profit off the people who continue to use them.

single-member districts   Geographical units that select a sole representative for a legislative body.

slander   Untrue statements harmful to a person's reputation that are communicated orally.

slate   A party's list of candidates for multiple offices.

social welfare policy   Governmental policies intended to improve the causes and effects of poverty.

Socialist party   Left-wing political party active in the early 20th century; generally supported an aggressive redistribution of wealth.

sound bite   A short remark by a politician that fits well into broadcast news stories.

Southern strategy   Richard Nixon's law-and-order emphasis when running for president; used to attract votes in the Southern states.

special committees   See *select committees.*

special envoys   Individuals engaging in diplomatic communications on the president's behalf who do not require Senate confirmation.

spin   The slant placed on political news by individuals with a vested interest in how the public interprets the news.

split ticket When voters select candidates from different parties for different offices.

spoils system System in which government employees are selected for party loyalty and replaced when a new administration takes power.

stagflation The condition of both high unemployment (stagnation) and inflation.

standing committees Permanent legislative committees that sift through proposed legislation.

stare decisis Doctrine that compels a court to build on precedent, letting previous decisions stand.

State's Rights party Primarily Southern political party used as a vehicle to challenge President Truman's civil rights program in 1948.

states' rights Idea that federal encroachment on state powers is a constitutional violation.

statutory interpretation When a court must interpret the meaning of laws passed by a legislature.

strict scrutiny When federal courts will permit a law only if it implements a "compelling government interest"; usually applied in cases involving race or religion.

subcommittees Legislative groups smaller than whole committees responsible for very specific areas of law.

suffrage The right to vote.

superior courts The first level of state trial courts, usually organized by county.

supremacy clause Constitutional provision declaring national law to be supreme across the United States.

tabloid press The "supermarket papers" that carry on the tradition of yellow journalism in modern times.

tariffs Taxes on goods imported into the country; the main source of federal revenue before the 20th century.

term limits Restrictions on how long a public official may serve.

Three-Fifths Compromise Helped settle the Constitutional Convention's debate over slavery. Slaves would be treated as $^3/_5$s of a person for determining a state's tax burden and number of representatives.

total incorporation A belief that the states may not violate any provisions of the first eight amendments of the Bill of Rights; has never enjoyed the support of a Supreme Court majority.

trade associations Economic interest groups that represent an entire industry.

Truman Doctrine Committed the United States to protecting "free peoples" of Europe from attack.

trustees Representatives who see their job as using their best judgment when voting.

unanimous consent agreement An agreement to which everyone consents on when to debate a bill.

unemployment rate The percentage of people in the labor force who lack jobs.

unfunded mandates Legislative requirement placed upon state and local government by Congress for which no funding is provided.

unicameral A legislature with only one chamber.

Union party   Republicans reorganized themselves as the Union party in 1864 to attract votes from the War Democrats.

unitary government   System of government in which a central authority holds all power.

universal manhood suffrage   A term used to signify that all men could vote, regardless of wealth or religion. When first coined, the term did not apply to African Americans.

value-added tax   A national sales tax that would impact products at each stage of their production.

Virginia Plan   James Madison's proposal for a new plan of government at the Constitutional Convention.

Voting Rights Act of 1965   Took numerous measures to ensure that racial minorities would enjoy full voting rights; banned literacy tests, required federal marshals to register voters in some counties, and regulated how some states could draw legislative districts.

War Powers Act of 1973   Attempt by Congress to limit the President's power to send American troops into combat; requires the president to get congressional approval if American troops are to be on foreign soil for 60 days or more.

welfare state   System in which the national government assumes major responsibility for social conditions.

Whig party   A 19th-century political party; it was one of the two major parties until breaking up in the 1850s. Supported an active national government.

whips   Legislative leaders who whip their party members into line on votes.

white flight   When whites leave a neighborhood or school system to avoid integration.

White House Office   The president's main support personnel, including secretaries and lawyers.

winner-take-all elections   Contests in which the candidate with the most votes takes an office, and the votes for losing candidates do not make a difference.

World Bank   An international organization that assists developing economies by providing loans and technological assistance.

World Trade Organization (WTO) Used by the United States to open foreign markets to American goods and protect American patents abroad.

writ of certiorari   A request to the Supreme Court that it review a decision made by lower courts.

yellow journalism   Sensational approach to selecting and reporting news, popularized by William Randolph Hearst.

INDEX